That's My Opinion, Period!

That's My Opinion, Period!

Christopher Greco

authorHOUSE®

AuthorHouse™
1663 Liberty Drive
Bloomington, IN 47403
www.authorhouse.com
Phone: 1-800-839-8640

First published by AuthorHouse   07/12/2011

ISBN: 978-1-4634-3400-7 (sc)
ISBN: 978-1-4634-3399-4 (dj)
ISBN: 978-1-4634-3398-7 (ebk)

Library of Congress Control Number: 2011912137

Printed in the United States of America

Any people depicted in stock imagery provided by Thinkstock are models, and such images are being used for illustrative purposes only.
Certain stock imagery © Thinkstock.

This book is printed on acid-free paper.

Preface

I would like to thank all of the people that have influenced me throughout my 24 years of life. Without them I would not have had the experiences and memories that make me who I am today. In one way or another each person has taught me a different value or lesson in life, whether it was good or bad. For that I am truly grateful to have met and gotten to know each one of you and am truly blessed to have the people that mean the most to me in my life today and in the days to come.

Now I am not going to lie to you. I actually just erased most of this part because this was one of the first things I did before I wrote the book. Looking at this book-"That's My Opinion, Period!"-this is more of a book on how to look at different values from a different perspective. Basically, this is a book of my opinions and should be viewed as such. In no way, shape, or form am I making any "facts" about life or certain situations (whether they are hypothetical or from my own experiences). For the people that read this book, know that the thoughts and things that I have experienced are from my own opinion and experiences from my own personal life. They are not opinions or experiences from someone else. Yes there are some of my experiences that mention other people who have been in my life and again, are from my own personal thoughts and conclusions. If for any reason you do not like what is written in this book then simply do not read it. You have to make the choice whether to read this book or not.

This book talks about what I believe are the most important values people should apply to their own lives. Some chapters are more about different things (politics, religion, economics, etc.) and again are from my own personal opinions about these topics and should not be taken to heart. There are no "set in stone" facts I write about for any of these topics, but simply how I look at them. People who read this book should read this book because they want a different perspective on life and are looking for someone else's opinion on things that they may have questions about.

As a result, this book again is for anyone who wants a different opinion on life or maybe they are looking for a question to be answered. I personally believe that this book is really intended for the youth of America. With so many questions and thoughts about life and how they should go about living it, I wanted to inspire the youth of America with my own personal thoughts and opinions on values and certain topics of interest. Being young myself as I mentioned above, I feel that I have lived a lot of life in my 24 years and want to give something to the youth of America in return. I want to be able to not only voice my opinion in this book but also inspire and teach others to do great and wonderful things, not only for themselves, but for others around them as well!

The chapters in this book range from values such as respect and responsibility to love and laughter. The topics again vary from politics and economics, to religion and addictions. There are things in this book that may not be suitable for young children and in no way is meant for them. This book should be used by youth who are a year or two away from venturing out into the real world. Then again, maybe this book helps inspire an even younger crowd of children to go and do great and wonderful things as well. If parents see fit to expose this book to their children then that is by all means their choice. As adults, you should be able to take responsibility for allowing your children to read or not to read this book. Understand that this book is written in the mind of a 24-year-old and has language and experiences that some children may not fully understand or even confuse them more. Again, as parents and adults, you need to make the choice on whether or not your children read this book or not.

In this book, I try to explain to the reader the true power of these everyday values and how they can help them to not only be great, but to also do great things. Again, this is an opinionated book about these values and topics and may not apply to people who do not have an open mind. This book explains that all people are different and may do certain things for a reason. That it is okay to be who you are and to accept you for you. To understand how to treat others and treat yourself in a positive manner. That it is okay to take responsibility for your actions and choices whether they are good or bad and to more importantly, accept responsibility for your choices and actions. To respect others for their different opinions whether you believe them to be right or wrong. Above all, to laugh, love, and show loyalty to not only yourself, but others as well. Finally that by making good choices, you not only set yourself up for successes, but you also make a better world for yourself and others as well.

So here it is-the book based solely on my opinion and nobody else's. The book that was inspired by me to enlighten others and to bring a different perspective to the table. A book that was created to help others understand and realize that there is truly something bigger than themselves out there. So again, here it is-the book "That's My Opinion, Period!" Enjoy!

Special Thanks

I know that this book was not just the work from me, but all of those who have had an effect on my life to make me think and act the way I do (whether good or bad). I would like to thank the following people for making a difference in my life and ultimately inspiring me to write this book in the first place.

My mother, Lynn, and my father, Donald, for teaching me right from wrong and allowing me to learn from their mistakes. My grandmother, Gertrude (Mimay), for teaching me it's okay to voice your opinion even if others don't accept you for it. My sisters, Janelle and Brandy, for allowing me to learn from their mistakes. My Aunt Jan and Uncle Paul Prenoveau for teaching me it's okay to think and do what is in your heart even if others around you do not accept you for who you are or what you do. My Aunt Fran for teaching me it's okay to think outside the box and to teach others to do the same. My best friend and "brother" Shadow, who taught me how to be loyal even if it means taking the heat for something you did not do. To my good friend, U.B., for teaching and showing me how true friends act towards one another and how friends should be there for you whether you are having a good day or bad day. To Kenny for teaching me how to be determined in what you do and how to be strong with your mind, body, and emotions no matter what the situation is. To one of my good friends and "brothers," Charlie, for showing me life can be full of laughter and joy if you can accept your mistakes and show others how to joke about them as well. To my Uncle Paul Brown who taught me that life is about being able to laugh and enjoy, even in our darkest hours. To the students of Unadilla Valley Central School who inspire me day in and day out and show me that there is indeed a bright future for America! To the teachers and staff of Unadilla Valley Central School for showing me not only how to learn, but how to teach and inspire others as well. To Jenifer for showing me how friends should act towards one another. To my friends, Brian and Noe, for showing me how everyday people should act and treat others whether they know them or not and no matter what their differences may be. Finally, to all the family, friends, and ultimately everyone and everything that I have missed for teaching and showing me many things in my life whether they were good or bad. You have all truly inspired me!

Opinions

I wanted this topic to be the very first chapter in this book. Not because that is what the book is mainly about or that it is part of the title of this book, but to help you the reader to better understand that everyone has their own. It's not a matter of voicing out your opinion all the time, but listening to other peoples' opinions as well. I believe that everybody wants to be heard. As a result, nobody really wants to listen to other peoples' opinions. Now don't get me wrong; I am sure that there are some people out there that listen more than they speak out. If you are one of those people who tend to listen more, then take this chapter as understanding that there are people out there who would rather be heard instead of simply listening from time to time.

There is nothing wrong with being heard. A lot of people have had great and wonderful ideas. Some people inspire others to think differently or to look at certain things differently as a result of simply listening to other peoples' perspectives and opinions. However, being heard 24/7 is not the way to go through life. Whether you know that you are one of these people or not, understanding and accepting that you are indeed one of these people, will lead you faster to understanding that people around you also want to be heard as well. Let's say that you are someone who loves the attention that others show you and you love to be heard all the time as well, but hate to have to listen to someone go on and on about what they think. Do you think that people are going to continue to show you that attention you love so much if you do not show any interest in what they have to say? I'll answer that one: no. In my opinion and from what I have seen myself, I believe that people who act like this are the ones that are looked at by others as self-centered. They are more likely to be looked at as selfish than understanding. As a result, and again from what I have seen, people will slowly turn away from these self-centered people and focus their attention on people who show attention to their thoughts and ideas. Leaving a very lonely life for those who want it all, but don't want to give anything. So again, if you come to the realization that you are indeed one of these people, the "cure" is very simple. Just simply show others the attention that you yourself love so much. Remember, everyone wants to eventually voice their opinion and be heard as well. If you do not show the respect towards others and listen to their opinions, then plan on not being around them for too long.

Being able to voice your opinion is a great thing. It is what has helped our nation evolve and grow with great ideas. Imagine if Dr. Martin Luther King Jr. never spoke out about his opinions in the 1960's. This would be a very different world that we live in today. It is important to understand that by allowing people to voice their opinions, it allows others to think and come up with opinions on their own. I don't believe that when they were coming up with the space shuttle design that there was only one person with the correct idea. There were probably many different people with many different opinions on what would and would not work. The same goes for everybody in today's world. Whether you are doing something small or big, your opinion matters in ways that you could not even imagine. So it is always important to voice your opinion. It helps inspire others to think and come up with their own personal opinions.

Not for one minute think that this book was created based on my own opinions. It was with the help of everyday people who inspired me to think and understand in different ways that encouraged me to create this book. Now don't get me wrong, this book is based solely on my opinions of these values and topics, but I wouldn't have these opinions if I had never experienced them in one way or another. I would not have come up with chapters like respect or responsibility if I never heard other peoples' opinions on respect and responsibility. I would only have one mind set (or tunnel vision) on those two values along with the rest of the values in this book. It is imperative to understand that by simply listening to other peoples' opinions, it will open your mind to many new perspectives and opinions of your own. If no one ever told me their opinion on having a drive for something, I would think that having a drive would simply be to drive somewhere. But after my experiences, having a drive means having a passion to do something and willing to do anything to achieve it. So remember, voicing your opinion is good, but it may be even better to listen to other peoples' opinions as well.

You will go insane if you think that you'll always have the same opinion as someone else. I believe that no two people are the same in this world. Yes, some may agree with you on certain topics or ideas, but do not by any means count on people to always agree with you. You will be setting yourself up for disappointment all the time. Instead, you should come to the understanding that no two people are the same and that goes for their opinions as well. With regards to the space shuttle, I am pretty confident it was not just one person who had the correct design for the space shuttle, but many different minds worked together to create a final design. One person may have come up with how the wings should look while another came up with what material would be best to use. This same thought process is how you should look at many things including this book. Don't just look at something as "set in stone," but more of a different perspective on someone's opinion. Look at the chapters in this book as someone's different perspective and personal opinions on these values and topics. Come up and create your own opinions on these values and topics. Like many things in life, you're going to find out that not everything works for everyone. The same goes for the chapters in this book. I am not asking you to work on all of these values every single day. Take the values from this book and apply the ones you see fit when you feel you need to apply them into your life. Nobody is going to hold your hand through life and tell you when to be respectful or responsible. Nobody is going to hold your hand and say "listen to that person" or "you shouldn't believe that." As an adult, you need to understand that your opinion is the one that matters and that you have to know when your opinion should be voiced or silenced.

Knowing when to keep quiet about your opinion is key to being respectful towards others. Not everyone wants to hear what you have to say 24/7 so knowing when and where to voice your opinion is important. Maybe you don't like your boss and talk to a co-worker about how you don't like how your boss treats you. By voicing your opinion to your co-worker, you risk your boss finding out how you really feel about him. Maybe this co-worker has been friends with your boss since high school. Maybe this co-worker knows that you both are up for a promotion and by telling your boss how you really feel will give the co-worker the edge over you. This is just one of many examples, but my point is that it is important to know that voicing your opinion at the wrong time can actually hurt you more than it can help you. Maybe you know that someone is going to do something special for someone's birthday and you tell a friend. Again, you risk this friend blabbing to this person who is getting a surprise for their birthday. Maybe you are in a situation where someone has just lost a family member and you go up to her and give her your opinion on something, whatever it may be. Chances are she will not care what your opinion is on whatever it is you're talking about. Again, remember that not everyone is up for what you have to say 24/7 and knowing when to speak your opinion and when not to, is very important!

Like many things in life there is a time and place for everything, including when to voice your opinion and when to simply listen to someone else's opinion. Not everything in life is about you, so don't make it look that way. Show interest in other peoples' opinions before your own. Being able to voice your opinion can be a great and inspiring thing to do. It may give other people a different perspective on things that they wouldn't have otherwise thought about. Just like the space shuttle, it's not up to just one person's opinions or ideas to make something happen. It is more of having many different ideas and opinions on something to make it happen successfully. By understanding when to voice your opinion and when not to, you can show the greatest respect towards others and maybe learn something yourself in the process.

Having The Drive

Having the drive to do something may not always be the easiest thing to do. You have to have passion for it. Once the passion runs out, then what? You have to want it no matter what, even on the worst of days. I have learned that if you cannot put 110% into it, then you probably shouldn't be doing it in the first place. However, there may be times when you think you'll never have the drive to do something. Then out of the blue, you have so much passion for it, you feel like you have the drive to do whatever it takes to get it and keep it in your life. Many people think that in order to have the drive for something, it has to be something big, like becoming a famous actor or NASCAR driver, making a million dollars, and owning five homes. In my opinion, having the drive for something can be as simple as having the drive to make someone laugh who is having a bad day or is sick, or spending time with your grandmother or another family member. Don't get me wrong now, having the drive to do something big isn't wrong, but it's not the only thing to have a drive for. In my opinion, having the drive for everything you do in life will make you that much happier. Being able to look back and see what you have accomplished by putting 110% into everything, will give you a feeling of confidence as well as know-how. At least it has for me.

However, putting 110% into everything doesn't always have to work out for the best. Sometimes it may seem that you put 110% into something you do and you get no good feeling from it. When I was pursuing my dream of becoming a NASCAR driver (1998-2009), I learned quickly that I had to have the drive to do it or nothing would ever become of my dream. Whether it was my actions, ideas, or even my emotions, I had to make sure I was putting 110% into it. By believing and setting small goals for myself, I was able to go from racing go-karts locally in 2000 to testing a NASCAR Craftsman Truck in Hickory, NC, by 2007. Like I said before though, if you don't feel the passion for what you're doing or you are unable to put a 110% into something, then you probably shouldn't be doing it. That happened to my dream of racing in the very beginning of 2009. After I was involved in a really bad accident in December of 2008, I had a different feeling about my dream of becoming a NASCAR driver. I felt as if it wasn't as important to my life or what I wanted to do with my life. At this point I felt depressed knowing that I spent eleven years of my life pursuing something I ultimately did not want to do. I lost the drive to be a NASCAR driver and spent eleven years to come to that crossroads, but at least I tried. I was always afraid of having that feeling of "I wonder if…." If you find yourself asking the question "I wonder if . . ." then you probably should have at least tried.

None the less, having a drive for something is a great thing! I have learned that by having this feeling, you can accomplish anything. You have to feel it and want it. Ultimately that is what "having the drive" is. It's wanting something so badly that you put 110% into getting it no matter what the cost. Now take my dream for example. I had a lot of sacrifices in pursuing my dream. I gave up time with my family and friends, drove cross country for long hours, spent loads of money, had countless nights that I lay awake thinking about what I had to do the next day to get that much closer, etc . . . Knowing what I know now, I never would have done half, if not all, of those things, but I did because I had the drive to do whatever I needed to do to become that NASCAR driver. I had people asking me "why are you doing this?" or "why are you investing so much money into this?" No matter what I told them, they never understood why I did what I did. It was because I had the drive to get there. I was putting 110% into my dream no matter what.

Sometimes it is tough when you loose the drive to do something you wanted to do for most of your life. It has long been said however, "when one door closes, another one opens." After I moved back to my hometown, I had to stop and figure out what I was going to do with the rest of my life. I had to find something I was passionate about, something that would give my life meaning. I started working a few different jobs, but only one that has given me that drive to keep doing it. I started substituting at my local school and I now find myself passionate about being a part of so many different lives as well as making a difference in those lives as well. I love being able to go teach kindergarten one day and teach high school English the next. Being able to interact with not only the students in all the different grades, but the teachers and staff as well, has been inspirational. I have really gotten the drive to keep substituting and putting 110% into it. Sometimes that's what happens: "one door closes and another opens." My drive for becoming a NASCAR driver has died, but my passion to substitute and make a difference in this world has been born. If things hadn't happened to me as they did, I'd probably still be putting 110% into racing.

As I go through life, I have found that if you are passionate about accomplishing something, you should have the drive to go out there and do it. Not everything in life is going to work out. So if your drive for something dies, don't worry. I have found that worrying is one of the worst things you can do in any situation. It may lead to poor health issues or a bad attitude towards yourself and others. So before you go down this road, stop and ask yourself, "ok, what's next?" What are you passionate about now? Maybe you're not passionate about anything at this point. Maybe you have to wait and find it further down the road. But my main point is, don't worry that your life is now meaningless just because you lost your drive for something. Not everything in life is instantaneous like getting movies on demand or throwing something in the microwave and having it hot in seconds. You have to have patience and not rush through life.

Having the drive to do something means you are willing to put 110% into it no matter what. It is better to try something then to never try it at all. Never leave yourself asking the question "I wonder if…." Sometimes it's hard when you lose the drive for something you were once so passionate about. "When one door closes, another one opens." Be patient in looking for something you are passionate about or want to have a drive for. Not everything in life is instantaneous and neither is finding something to be passionate about.

Trusting Yourself First

This chapter says a lot about your character and your beliefs. I'm not specifically talking about religion or whether or not you have good character traits or bad ones. More about whether you trust yourself. Would you trust yourself with a heavy decision that had to be made? Would you trust yourself to make the right decision even if the decision you had to make would benefit you and hurt someone else? Would you trust yourself before you would trust someone else? All pretty good questions and at first glance you would probably answer all of them with the best moral answer, but would that be true? A lot of people feel as if they do the right thing no matter what and can trust themselves to do so. But what makes something right and what makes something wrong? For this question to be answered, you have to ask yourself that. It's what makes us understand right from wrong.

Do you trust yourself? Most people answer "yes." However, most of these people would ask friends, colleagues, or family members what they think only because they do not trust themselves to have the correct answer. When taking a closer look at the question, we come to realize that there is no correct answer, but only one answer that works for you in that given situation. Let me give you an example. Let's say you got sick and had both a fever and sinus problems. You know that you can either take Ibuprofen to reduce the fever or take Nyquil to reduce the sinus problem. So you ask someone, what should I take? Now I'm not saying that asking for someone's opinion about which one to take is a problem, but it boils down to which one you want to get rid of first: the fever or the sinus problem. You have to trust in yourself that you will make the best decision for you.

Maybe you realize that by thinking about it and feeling how you do, you decide that going to the doctor is the best route for you. Maybe someone would suggest that, but then again, maybe they wouldn't. That is why when it comes to decision-making, it is okay to ask for someone's opinion, but you have to trust in yourself that ultimately, you will make the right decision for you.

I use to work at a pharmaceutical plant close to where I live. There were a lot of heavy decisions that had to be made daily. Many times you didn't have the time to ask for someone's opinion on something. Whether it was completing one order before another or determining whether you had enough room to dump a barrel of medicine into the hopper. Being able to get the training I got, I was able to make these decisions on my own. Sometimes I didn't have any training on some things. For example, it was difficult to trouble shoot or clean a piece of machinery I had never been trained on. First, I knew that I had to go over the proper documentation for that specific piece of machinery. Then, I had to follow the step-by-step procedure on how to clean or trouble shoot that piece of machinery. Above all, I had to double-and triple-check my work that I had done. By knowing what I had to do and how I had to do it, I could trust myself to do the job right. It was imperative that I trust myself before asking someone else. What if I asked for someone's opinion and he had told me to clean or trouble shoot the piece of machinery a certain way and it ended up being the wrong way? It would have been my decision to do it the way he told me to do it and ultimately, it would have been my fault because I made the choice to trust someone else before myself. You have to be able to trust yourself to make the big and heavy decisions in life on your own. Should I go to college for mechanical engineering or for political science? Neither at this time. Should I buy a truck or a car? A car would be the better choice for me. Do I need to save for my next car payment or mortgage payment? Both but how can I do that? All these questions and more I can almost guarantee you will have to not only ask yourself, but make a decision solely on your thoughts and ideas.

Being able to trust yourself is not only being able to make the tough decisions on your own, but being able to trust yourself to make the right decisions instead of the wrong ones. In 2008 I was in a relationship with the love of my life. I had given up my job at the pharmaceutical plant, left my family and old life behind, all to start a family of my own. I felt like this was it. My life was perfect. I trusted in myself that I had made the right decision. Or did I? We were ten years apart in age. She was divorced with three children from her previous marriage and was living with her parents (until she got a place of her own). I may have trusted myself that I made the right decision but ultimately, I made a decision based on what I wanted to think was right. If I had looked at the facts and been honest with myself and trusted my gut reaction from that, I most likely would not have given up everything for something that ultimately did not work out at all. That is what you're going to have to do in life as well. Being able to decide what is right and what is wrong. You may think that something that sounds good is right for you, but if you do not have all the facts about it then how can you trust yourself to make the right decision? I'll answer that one: you cannot. Before jumping right into something, ask yourself, "How will this affect my life? Will anyone get hurt from it physically or emotionally?" Before you answer those two or any other questions that you might come up with, you absolutely have to have the facts first! Without the facts, you will never be able to trust yourself to make the right decision. If I had had all the facts and thought about them, I would have never gotten into that relationship. But because I did not think about the facts that I had, I made the wrong decision for the right reason. I wanted to be in a relationship and start a family. By choosing the wrong person and time to do so, it was the wrong decision for me. Ultimately, I trusted myself that I had made the right decision when in fact, I made the wrong decision. You have to trust in yourself that you will make the right decisions for the right reasons and you do that by having all of the facts.

To sum up, you have to trust yourself to make the best decision based on what you know and how you feel. You have to trust yourself first, before you can trust someone else's opinion. You must trust yourself to make the right decision for the right reason. In order to trust yourself to make the right decision you have to have all of the facts about the decision you need to make.

Laugh!

aughing is probably one of the most important things you can do throughout your day. Laughing brings you joy, happiness, smiles, and much more. Unfortunately most people today do not laugh on a daily basis. Some situations are understandable such as the death of a loved one, the loss of job, or an accident. But even the most solemn situations are sometimes the best times to laugh. You just have to learn and know when to laugh and when not too. As stupid as that sounds, it's very true. In some situations you probably should not laugh or try to make someone laugh. You could offend them or make an idiot out of yourself. However, as in many things in life, if there are certain times not to laugh, then there are certain times to laugh. You just have to figure out when that time is. You're not always going to be right and you will most likely find yourself in a situation where you offended someone without knowing it at first or make yourself look like that idiot that you didn't want to look like. That is just part of life and how you learn.

It sounds absolutely stupid to have to "pick and choose" when to laugh and when not too. For now, lets figure out why. I'll give you an example and hopefully you can make the connection from there and apply it to situations in your own life. Let's say that Billy and you always joke, laugh, and have a good time. You two have worked with each other at the same job for the past two years. You heard about an embarrassing experience that one of your boss's had with another employee. You finally catch up to Billy and notice that he is walking with his head down, kind of mopey looking. You're not getting that happy-go-lucky feeling when you see Billy walking up the hall. You mention to Billy about the embarrassing story about your boss. Billy then replies, "that's not very nice" and keeps walking up the hall away from you. So now what?

Most likely Billy was having a bad day which is pretty obvious by all the signs he gave (walking with his head down, mopey looking, not getting a good "vibe"). You probably should not have said anything, except "is everything ok?" Remember everybody is different and not everybody is up for a good laugh 24/7. Everybody has their own lives to live and some days are just worse than others. Maybe Billy had a death in the family or he had gotten a ticket and lost his license yesterday after work. Maybe Billy was involved with your boss's embarrassing moment and had his job threatened. Your best bet is to find out what is wrong with Billy before you go telling funny stories or cracking jokes like always. Now that was just one way your situation could have turned out. Maybe telling Billy that funny story makes him laugh and brightens the rest of his day. My point is there is a time and a place for everything, including laughing. Not everyone is looking to laugh 24/7 and you have to know when the right time is.

Now laughing at everyday situations is something I try to do. I never use to do this. I use to laugh or try to make people laugh to have them like me or look cool. The reality of it is (or at least in my opinion), you should laugh because something is funny or amuses you. Not just for the sake of looking cool or trying to make people laugh. Trying to make someone laugh to bring joy or happiness into their day is great. Just make sure it is all for the right reasons. This should be the only reason you make someone laugh. Not for your own personal benefit (in other words making yourself look better at someone else's expense). Obviously that is my opinion and should be taken that way. However, with the number of jobs I have had in various states throughout my life thus far, and no matter where I work, one of the many constants I find is people who make fun of or belittle someone else to make a joke or to make themselves look better. That is the point I am trying to make here. You should not go out to get a cheap laugh at someone else's expense. Not only does that hurt whoever you are talking about, but it does not make you look any better either. If anything, joke about yourself before others. I find myself doing that more and more each day and it puts a smile on everyone's face without hurting anyone's feelings or making myself look like an idiot. Obviously you shouldn't cut yourself down or belittle yourself if you're not in the mood or have had a bad day, but I suggest joking about your own life before making someone else look like a joke for your own benefit.

Making sure that it is the right time and place to make someone laugh can be a great thing! Bringing joy to someone else's life and uplifting their day not only brings happiness to your own life, but gives you a better outlook on your own life. Imagine if everyone in the world today laughed about events that happened in their own life on a daily basis. You'd see a lot more people simply enjoying life. I'll give you an example from this past week at work. I was substituting for a music teacher at the local school. My day started off with loud middle school kids and then a trip to the restroom in between my 6th and 7th grade classes. I ended up dropping my I.D. badge in the toilet (while the toilet was as clean as possible). From there I went and had lunch duty in the cafeteria for 5th grade where I had to raise my voice and send a student to the principal's office for using foul language (while he was standing 5 yards away from 1st and 2nd graders). Finally I ended my day escorting a kindergarten student down to the office for yelling at me and sticking his tongue out at me. With all these events that happened throughout my day, I had two choices I could have made. I could have been disappointed and looked at this as being a crappy day, making myself miserable or I could have just simply laughed about all the different events and said "oh well, tomorrow's Friday and pay day!" A few years ago having days like this one, I would have chosen the first choice, wondering to myself "why can't I have a good day everyday?" This time however, I choose the second option and enjoyed making my grandmother and mother laugh when I told them (in a joking manner) about my wonderful Thursday. You see, you can go through life feeling miserable about each day and have an end result of feeling like your life is crappy and meaningless or you can laugh at the events that happen throughout each day and have your end result of feeling good about being able to laugh at your experiences and make others laugh and enjoy their own life in the process. Each one of your days is never going to be perfect so when it comes right down to it, ultimately it's your choice to laugh over it or be miserable about it.

Laughing is one of the most important things you can do throughout our day. Although it sounds extremely stupid, knowing when to laugh and when not to is key to not only making yourself feel good, but the people around you feel good as well. There is a time and a place for everything, including laughing and joking around. Joke about your own life and experiences before making a joke of someone else's life or experiences. Making yourself or someone else laugh should be about bringing joy and happiness to your own life as well as everyone's lives around you.

Think Positively

In the previous chapters I have touched on this subject in different forms. All of us, including myself, don't think positively 24/7. Just imagine if we did. You'd have a lot of people in this world feeling complete and confident in themselves. Now don't get me wrong. There are a lot of people that think positively throughout their day. However, there are many more people who don't thing positively than those that do. Why is that? For starters, a lot of people that think positively were brought up that way. I'm not saying that you have to have a perfect childhood to have a positive outlook on life, but you have to have had a positive childhood experience to have a positive outlook on life.

In my opinion most people who have had a good childhood will have a positive outlook on life, while most people who had a rough childhood will most likely not have a positive outlook on life. By a rough childhood, I mean that maybe the child was neglected, abused, or treated poorly. Maybe the child was taught that life is tough. The rich get richer and the poor get poorer. You will never achieve your goals. In my opinion, children that look at their parent's lives at a very young age tend to follow in their footsteps. Now I am not telling people how to raise their children or how to be better parents. I'm just saying I have seen children who have great outlooks on life and those children who have no positive outlook at all. They have to learn it from someone and since they don't have the same teachers or friends in their lives year after year after year, the only constant is whoever they live with at home. Again I am not telling anyone to follow my advice, but in my opinion if you do nothing else in your life, make sure to have a positive outlook on a child, whether it's your child or someone else's! Children follow by example and if you show them that it's good to have a positive outlook on life, then chances are they will grow up looking at life in a positive way.

I have found that thinking positively is not always an easy task. You're always questioning yourself whether it's right or wrong, whether it's fair or unfair, etc. I have found that if you think in a positive way, then you'll always receive positive results. Like everything in life I have also found that if you think in a negative way, then you'll always receive negative results. I'll give you an example. Have you ever gotten up in the morning and started off the day with either stubbing your toe or spilling your drink? What did you think after that? Most people would answer this by saying "my day just went downhill from there." That's because they thought in a negative way. You stub your toe and think to yourself, "oh great, what else will go wrong today?" and before you know it, you're at the end of your day and you feel like you had a crappy day. If you only thought to yourself after stubbing your toe, "Wow, that hurt! Let's not do that again!" or laughed about it, you would not have put too much thought into having a crappy day to begin with. If you think positively about stubbing your toe instead of negatively, chances are you're less likely to look at the rest of your events throughout your day in a negative way. As a result you'll change your negative crappy day into a positively good day. It can be that simple!

Since many people were brought up as looking at life as a big challenge, then chances are they will think that they have to struggle through life just to make it through. Here's the reality of life. Nobody makes it through life alive! Have you ever heard about somebody surviving life? No, and chances are if you ever do, you'll hear about it on "The Today Show" or "Nightly News." Not to stray to far from the topic, if nobody gets out of life alive, then why go through life thinking negatively? Why don't you make the most of it and think positively about your life and the world around you? Not only will you feel better about yourself, but you'll most likely make the people around you feel positive as well. Remember, it's the simplest things in life that make for a great world to live in! Thinking positively will give you the confidence you need to do great things and make for a better world around you. Imagine if everyone did this. Ultimately, if we started a chain reaction of people thinking and doing positive things, this would be a great and positive world to live in!

Feeling complete comes with making positive choices throughout your day. Instead of not helping someone because you feel lazy and don't want to use the energy, think of different ways to help that person out and you'll most likely find yourself motivated to step up and lend a hand. As a result, you'll feel like you accomplished something out of your day and make yourself feel complete. It all starts with thinking about doing something positive and then acting upon your thought. If your day is all about sitting on a couch watching reruns of a show, then that's a waste of your time and energy. However, if your day is spending time with your grandmother watching reruns of a show she likes, then you're going out of your way to make her feel wanted. Let's say that your grandmother spends her day sitting on a couch doing crosswords and watching T.V. because she has limited mobility and can't walk downtown or drive anywhere. Then by going out of your way to spend your time with your grandmother, you make her feel wanted and not alone. Although you're just sitting there watching T.V. with her and chit-chatting about whatever, you're making her day feel like it's worth something instead of making her think to herself "what am I doing with myself?" or "why am I still here?" or even "what's the point in living still?" It's creative positive thinking like that that makes even your grandmother feel like she has something to look forward to during her day. Maybe you get closer to your grandmother during her last years of life instead of avoiding her and wasting that time you have with her. All because you thought of spending time with her (using positive thinking). You made her last years of her life go from a meaningless void into a meaningful life. It's that simple!

Confidence comes from many things including thinking positively. If you can't think positively about anything, then chances are you won't have the confidence to do much of anything. Let's say you have an important deadline to get a product out the door at work. You know it will take a good two days to get the product out the door, but the bosses want you to get the product out the door in a day and a half. If you don't think positive about getting that product out the door, then most likely you won't have the confidence in making it happen. By thinking positively about the task, maybe you also start thinking about different ways to make it happen. Maybe you can save some time by working a different way or using a different procedure instead of the normal one you use. By doing your work differently, you save a whole day and get the product out in a day instead of the normal two days it would have taken the other way. By thinking positively about your deadline, now you found a way to save countless hours using a different procedure during each work day. You are promoted or given a raise. If you thought of your deadline in a negative way, chances are you would have worried yourself, and possibly the rest of your co-workers, into messing something up and causing you to lose more time when you could have saved time by thinking positively. Again, it's that simple!

By thinking positively you can gain confidence and a sense of completeness in your life. Although all of us do not think positively 24/7, doing so as much as possible will set us up for successes each and every day. Having a positive outlook on life can start from as young as your childhood so it's probably best to make sure that we show our youth that it's good to think positively! Teaching your children to have a positive outlook on life will most likely send them in the right direction. Think positively about certain events that start off your day and it can lead to a better day for you. Nobody gets out of life alive, so why go through life thinking negatively? By thinking positively and acting upon those thoughts, you'll make a better world for yourself and those around you. It's the simplest things in life like thinking positively that make for a great and better world to live in!

Pace Yourself

Over the course of my life thus far (24 years), I have found that if you rush things, almost all the time they don't turn out the way you want them to. Chances are if you find yourself rushing around trying to work at something to get it done so you get to the result you want faster, then you most likely shouldn't be doing it in the first place. Whether it's at work, in your personal life, or anywhere, there are a lot of people out there that will try to rush you. That's when you have to decide, first of all, whether or not whatever it is, is worth doing in the first place. If you have to rush to get what you're after instead of going about it at your own pace, believe me when I say, it's not worth it. You have to live your own life at your own pace, not at someone else's. Just because someone else can do it faster (whatever it may be), doesn't mean you have to do it fast to get the same results.

Maybe you're one of the people that can do something at a faster pace than others. That's not a bad thing. What is bad is pushing someone else to do it at your pace and expect them to keep up. You should never push someone to do something at a faster pace. It brings frustration, anger, disappointment, and probably much more. If that happens, then chances are whatever it is that you want them to accomplish at your pace will take even longer due to the frustration, anger, and disappointment. Let people learn and work at their own pace! It will bring on better results as well as more confidence once they accomplish whatever it is they want or are asked to do. I mean let's say it takes you three months to learn Spanish but it takes Billy six months. Does that make Billy worse off or dumber than you? Not at all. It just means that Billy is learning at his own pace, which in this case takes him longer to learn Spanish. Maybe Billy can put together an engine in one month where it would take you two months to put that engine together. Does that make you worse off or dumber than Billy? Again, not at all. Working and learning at your own pace is the key to getting great results no matter what you're doing.

I see it all the time at school. Whether I am in Pre-K or 12th grade, all the students learn at their own pace. However, I see the students that take a longer time to learn, feeling down about themselves or frustrated that they can not learn the material like the other students in their class. They feel dumber than the other students and as a result take even longer to learn the material just because they feel like they are behind. Sometimes even the teachers themselves get frustrated because certain students are not "up to speed" with where the rest of the class is. This is why schools need so many teacher aides in all grades. They don't need them because the school has an extra $200,000 they needed to spend. Students need the extra help because they all learn at their own pace. When I was in school, I remember certain times when I felt like I was falling behind because I couldn't keep up the pace with the other students in my class. You just have to take your time and learn and work at your own pace. It may feel torturous at first, but once you figure out what pace you learn at, it makes life easier.

I find that working out is a great place to start when teaching yourself to pace yourself. A lot of times people see celebrities or models on television and value how great their bodies look. Then they get discouraged when they look at themselves in the mirror. People set high goals for themselves that are too "out of reach." Then when they don't get to where they want to be, they get even more discouraged with themselves. In my opinion, you need to work out by just pacing yourself and starting off slowly and working up to a faster pace. The results will be ten times better than if you just jump right into working out at that faster pace. This is why most people get discouraged with themselves when starting to work out (whether it's the first time or tenth time). People think that if they do one hundred sit-ups and push-ups everyday for a month that they'll end up with the six pack abs and incredible arm muscle. This is not the case. By pacing yourself when you first start working out (let's say ten sit-ups and ten push-ups), they'll have the confidence in a couple of weeks to up the number of sit-ups and push-ups. Before you know it you're six months into working out and up to sixty or seventy sit-ups and push-ups. Another thing you need to pace yourself at when working out is the number of days you actually work out. Since your body is not use to you working out seven days a week, most people will actually hurt themselves by simply working out too much. By starting out one to two days a week and working up from there, you're better off and less likely to pull muscles or hurt yourself. By applying the simple act of pacing yourself (whether it's working out or learning Spanish) you can not only accomplish your task at your own comfortable pace, but most likely you'll learn or achieve better results than if you were to rush at a faster pace.

People work and learn at their own pace. You may be able to learn and work at a faster pace, but that shouldn't mean you push someone to learn or work at your pace. When I was living down south I had a boss that wanted work done at his own pace. If you want to achieve something at your own pace, then chances are you should be doing it yourself. Most of the time I saw that two things were happening to the work that needed to be completed. Either the work was done so fast and quickly, that it ended up being very poor work or the work wasn't able to be completed at all. This was due to work that the boss wanted to be completed at his own pace and he expected others to keep up to his pace of work. Chances are if this man had given his workers more time to complete the task, then not only would the work have been completed on time, but the work would have been completed with quality. Make sure that you always give yourself enough time to learn what you need to learn or to get your work done at your own pace. Not only will you actually accomplish your task, but chances are you'll be done before your deadline is up and with better results.

By pacing yourself you can build confidence in yourself as well as better results. It's never a good idea to push someone or even yourself to a faster pace. You may be able to learn or work at a faster pace than others, but give others more time to learn and work at their own pace. Just because you learn or work at a slower pace than others doesn't mean you're worse off or dumber than others. Not everyone works and learns at your pace and you don't learn and work at everyone else's pace. It's something you have to find out on your own because everyone is different and that means that everyone goes at their own pace.

Believe and Have Faith

Believing and having faith doesn't necessarily mean that you have to be religious. Believing can be a part of anyone's life whether it's believing in yourself, others, a promise, etc. The same goes for having faith and that is why I put the two together in this chapter. They both are just about the same no matter how you look at it. Believing and having faith can be applied in many things, but you have to have both in order to trust yourself and others around you. You are not always going to believe in or have faith in someone or something. Maybe someone close to you has lied to you or talked behind your back and you found out about it. Does that mean you don't believe in them anymore or have faith that they will not lie to you or talk about you behind your back again? Maybe you now believe that you can not trust them or that you have faith that they will do it again. Faith is not always meant to be a "plus" for someone, but more about how you look at certain people, situations, or events at different times in your life.

Believing that you'll get the job or promotion and having the faith that you can do the work to get there are very positive outlooks you should have. This is true not just on your job or for a promotion, but everything in life. Believing that someone or the bus will be there on time so you can get where you need to be is another example. However, like everything in life, if there are positive beliefs then there must be negative ones. Having a negative belief about something is not always a bad thing. It's what makes you, you. If you believe that someone who has lied to you twice will lie to you again, then you're probably right. By believing that this person who has lied to you twice will lie to you again doesn't make you a bad person, just a wiser one. If they are aware of what they are doing and are trying to be a better person by not lying to you, then maybe you believe that they will indeed become a better person and not lie to you anymore. Like I said, your beliefs are what make you, you. Maybe you believe that your favorite football team will win the Super Bowl or that you'll be involved in a loving relationship by the end of the month. These are all positive and all very good beliefs, but again, they're your beliefs and not someone else's and that's what makes you, you.

Having faith is very similar to believing in something or someone. Having faith is (in my opinion) believing something will happen or someone will do something. As in the previous example if someone lies to you twice, then you may have faith that that same person will lie to you again. If there are negative thoughts of faith, then there must be positive thoughts of faith. Let's say you are doing great in school and you are getting good marks on all your work. Most likely you will have faith that you will pass the class or even pass with all A's. Maybe you meet someone that you are attracted to and now you have that feeling that you want to get to know them better and see if you're a match for each other. By having faith that it will work, you'll be thinking about all the positive things about a relationship with that person and most likely have that relationship with her. Watch out though. If there are positives, then there are negatives as well. If you only have faith in negative thoughts about that very same relationship, then chances are the relationship will not work because all you have faith in are the negative ones regarding that relationship. Like the chapter that talked about being positive, if you're always positive, then most likely you'll always have positive results. Same goes for being negative. If all you have are negative thoughts, then chances are you'll always get negative results. So if you always have positive beliefs and faith, you are more likely to have positive thoughts and positive results.

You don't have to be religious to believe or have faith in anything, but having a religious outlook on life is not always a bad thing either. In fact over the course of my life, I have found that people who believe in God and have faith that He exists have had a better positive outlook on life in general than those who do not believe or have faith in God. Maybe it's because the people who don't believe, don't look at life the same way as those who do believe. I am not going to tell you that I have concrete evidence that there is a God (or not), but would you agree that there is something bigger than us out there? In my opinion I do believe that there is something bigger than us out there and I have faith that someday I will find out. You see, believing in God is the same as believing you'll get promoted to that better job within the company. If you believe it, then you have faith that it will happen. Whether you have faith in God (or your job) you believe that it will happen. There are always positives and negatives in life. Since there are people who believe and have faith in God, then there are those who do not believe in or have faith in God. That doesn't make those people bad people. They are individuals that have their own beliefs and faiths. Maybe they believe that aliens were the ones responsible for life on Earth or maybe those people have faith that they'll prove that aliens were indeed the ones who we once perceived as gods.

Nobody should be looked down upon or be belittled for their beliefs or faiths. It is what makes us "us". It is what makes all of us independent and individuals because we can think, believe, and have our own personal faiths in whatever we choose. Here in America we have a lot more freedom to do this than many other countries due to the people who fought and the ones who continue to protect that right for us. I believe that without the freedom to think, act, believe, and have faith in whatever we want, it would be a much different world for us here in America. Imagine everyone believing in the same things and having faith in all the same things. What a boring place that would be. No one would speak out or believe in different things. Imagine if this was the case in the mid 20th century and people like Einstein, Dr. Martin Luther King Jr., or John F. Kennedy were not able to speak out about what they believed in or did not have that right. Yes, this would be a much different place if we did not have that right to believe and have faith in our own personal thoughts. Use your right to have the freedom to believe and have faith in whatever you want to believe in!

Everyone believes and has faith in their own personal thoughts which is what makes us "us." In life there are always going to be positives and negatives. The same goes for believing and having faith. You can have positive beliefs and faiths as well as negative beliefs and faiths. It's probably better to have positive beliefs and faiths instead of negative ones because the more positive things in our life, chances are the more positive results you'll get. Believing and having faith doesn't mean you have to be religious, but that doesn't mean you cannot be religious to believe and have faith either. Here in America we all have the right to believe and have faith in whatever we want (whether it's God, aliens, your job, or whatever) so let's use that freedom we have in the best positive way we can!

Patience

This is probably one of the most important chapters in this book. Not to say that any of the other chapters in this book are not just as important, but by having patience, you'll be able to accomplish great successes. In my opinion, being able to pace yourself requires much patience. There are a lot of people out there in the world today that don't use or have any patience whatsoever. Those impatient people end up frustrated with their lives and miserable all because they want the best results as fast as possible. When this does not happen for them, that is when the frustration comes in and as an end result, they're miserable. All this could have been prevented with the application of patience.

Learning how to have patience is probably one of the hardest learning curves for anyone in today's world. When you're surrounded by everyday technology and with life moving in such a fast pace, we find ourselves wanting everything in life to be fast-paced. As a result, this makes it harder for us to understand the real value of patience. You see, when things are done at a faster pace, we lose sight of what a little bit of patience will bring to the table. Spending more time doing something isn't always a bad thing. However, not all people understand this because we live in a fast-paced society. Maybe if everyone took their time, they'd give themselves time to think about what they're doing and do a better job at it. Because they were patient and took their time, they did the task ten times better than if they were to rush to slap it together. Maybe it's because people don't want to give their minds time to think about their lives and want to stay busy 24/7. Who knows? But the point is you'll enjoy life better and accomplish a lot more than if you were to have no patience.

When I was seeing my girlfriend back in 2008, we lived in different states and lived very different lives. I did not see this because I wanted my relationship with her to go from dating to something more serious. I wanted that family life with the wife, kids, pet, etc. and instead of being patient and letting things play out, I jumped right into it and moved out to where she was living. I gave up my $20 per hour job with full benefits, my family and friends, and pretty much everything, including my own way of life. A few months after I had moved and we decided to get engaged, I was working two jobs, bringing in about a hundred dollars less than what I was making back home. It seemed to be all falling apart. All of this could have been avoided by being patient and seeing how everything would have played out without moving and giving up everything in my life. My point is just because something seems good and you really want it, doesn't mean you should jump right into it. Wait, be patient, and look at all of your options. Once you see all the information, and envision how everything will play out in different scenarios, make your choice and stick with it. I know I could have saved myself a lot of heartache if I had been more patient in my decision making!

Not everything in life is going to be set right in front of you when you want it. By being patient and waiting for certain things in life to come to you, you'll receive better results than just going and jumping right into it. You should not be patient about everything in life. There are certain things you should be patient about consequently, there are certain things you should not be so patient about. I'm not saying date someone five years before committing to a serious relationship. I'm also not saying jump right into a relationship after you've known the person for two months either. This is where you need to make choices in your life. Nobody is going to stand behind you 24/7 making choices for you all the time. You're going to have to grow up and make these decisions on your own. Now maybe someone has some good advice for you, but then again maybe that advice is not so good either. You have to go and make your choice whether or not to take your time with something or just rush to get it done. Either way, take the time to decide whether you should be patient in your decision making or not.

Probably one of the greatest examples is in a sport that not too many people know how to do. Hunting is in my opinion one of the greatest ways to learn how to become patient. I know that I wasn't very patient when I first started out doing it, but I learned and got better at it and eventually became very good at it. I haven't been hunting in years, but if I went out there right this very second, I bet you it wouldn't take too long for me to get back into the swing of it. Hunting requires a lot of patience and there are a lot of hunters out there that are very impatient. I have heard many excuses for not going out hunting and some I even used myself. It got too cold out. There's nothing out there. It started to rain. There was too much noise in the woods. I spooked them. There are probably a million excuses out there, but the one hunter who always gets their game each and every year is the one who is the most patient hunter. Whether I was sitting or standing, I always got impatient when I first started hunting. My legs would get sore and cold. My hands and feet would do the same. I'd sit there for hours and hours and see nothing but the leaves blowing in the wind. After a couple of years however, I found the longer I sat and the quieter I was, the more chances I gave myself to see something. I was on a piece of property that no one else hunted during turkey season. I would walk around and see if I could find these elusive birds. I again found that if I was extremely quiet in my walking (taking a step and stopping . . . taking a step and stopping), looking with my ears instead of turning my head and seeing with my eyes (what I mean is, being able to hear something, identify it, and visualize what it is doing without being able to actually see it), I could actually sneak up on these birds without them knowing I was even there. My point is, if I never learned to be patient and learn different ways to go about hunting, I would have never set myself up for success. I would have always been discouraged and frustrated with my results and would have missed out on a great learning experience.

Between 2006 and 2008 I use to travel for my dream (becoming a NASCAR driver). I use to work 2nd shift (between 2:00 p.m. and 10:30 p.m.). After work I would drive from my work in New York all the way down to the track in North Carolina (12+ hour drive one way). You have to have a lot of patience driving long distances like that, especially after a full 8 hours of work. Normally I would sleep between 10-12 hours before I would go into work and make a trip like that (usually on a Friday). Because I was patient in my driving and didn't try to rush too much in getting there, I got to see a lot of the country and meet a lot of people along the way. I got to see the sun rise at 5 a.m. and see the sun set at 7 p.m. all in different states and sometimes even different time zones. When I moved to North Carolina in the middle of 2008, we made trips to races in many different states. From September to November I was on the road with the team 24/7 traveling all over the southern part of the United States. By being patient I got to enjoy parts of America and enjoy different company that I never would have been able to do if I was not patient. If I had been impatient I would have missed out on all of what this country is all about.

When I was in New York City for the first time, there were so many people and so many places I could have seen. Since I knew to be patient when I was there, I got to walk through some of the coolest places in the city and see some of its best features.

When I was in 6th grade, I was on our school's Safety Patrol. In May of every year the group would visit Washington, D.C. and Gettysburg, PA. During my trip there I wasn't patient. I wanted to see everything all at once. Years later when I helped chaperone the trip, I saw more and was able to soak more of it in because I had learned to be patient and take my time.

The same thing happened when I visited Walt Disney World in Florida. I went with my family last year and saw more frustrated, miserable children there than I ever expected. Why? Because they were so overwhelmed by everything and did not have the patience to go through a full day as an adult would. I even noticed some adults that were impatient as well. The point of all of this is that to really enjoy life to the fullest and soak in all the memories, you need to be patient and take your time with everything. In our fast-paced world, if you go through life at top speed, then chances are you'll miss out on all that life has to offer!

By being patient, you will have more time to think about your situation and make better choices after thinking about all of the possibilities you have. Learning to be patient is probably one of the hardest learning curves you'll ever learn, but it's worth it in the end. By being patient we have time to think and really soak in life's greatest gifts no matter what the situation. By being patient and seeing all of your options and envisioning the effect that each one will have, you are likely to make the right choice instead of the wrong one. Not everything in life is going to be given to you or set up for you. You have to make your own decisions and by being patient in your decision-making process, you have a better chance of setting yourself up for success!

Love

Love is one of the most important actions we can show to one another throughout our day. Love is what makes us want to be around one another and love is also what makes us want to do what we do. We wouldn't work at a job we didn't love, right? Chances are if we did we would not stay at that job too long. Same goes for loving one another. Now just so I make this clear, when I talk about loving one another, I don't mean having sex. Love is much more than just the physical part. Being able to love one another can range from being in an actual relationship to loving your family or friends. Showing that you love someone can also range from a hug or a kiss to helping one another with a task or just simply being there for them when they need you the most. Too many people in today's society believe that love is just being in a relationship, or being married, or just having sex. In fact you can show love during your day without being in a relationship, being married, or even having sex.

Showing love for your work or a hobby can be very moving and inspiring especially when you inspire someone else in the process. Due to some dreadful life experiences in 2008, I moved back to my hometown and was very depressed. I didn't feel like doing anything and was absolutely not motivated to accomplish anything. I just felt like curling up and dying to tell you the honest truth. It wasn't long after I moved back to my home town however that I started spending more time with my Grandmother (Mimay). In doing so I saw a show that would actually change my whole outlook on my current situation and life as well. The show had a main character who was going through some of the same situations I had gone through. By watching the show, I was able to learn how to deal with my depression and lift my spirits back up. I was able to do this because the actor loved what he was doing for his work. I could tell that he loved acting so much by the work that he did on this television series. That is actually what inspired me to pursue acting and give myself new life. If I can love my job like this actor loves his, then maybe I can inspire someone to do or be something just as great. That is what the power of love is all about. Being able to inspire someone to be or do something great!

Now love doesn't just mean you have to love your work. Love has many different forms that can be seen, heard, felt, even smelled and tasted. I absolutely love the smell of a Thanksgiving meal or the smell of cookies being baked. I love the taste of them as well. Love doesn't have to be just about relationships and sex (even though that is what most of society relates love to). You don't have to just show your love on Valentines Day. It can be a 24/7 addiction. In fact if you have to be addicted to anything, don't let it be alcohol or cigarettes; let it be love. Love the sound of a baby's laugh or the touch of your pet. I have had numerous pets that I absolutely loved. For me, animals seem to listen better and understand more than humans (obviously not all the time but when it counts the most). When I am happy and need someone to run around with and use up some energy with, I always go to our family dog and throw him a stick or frisbee. Maybe I need someone to talk to when I am sad, just to get my feelings out there. Animals don't butt in and tell you how to feel or how you should feel. They just listen to you no matter what you have to talk about. I absolutely love that about family pets. You see, love doesn't have to be just about being in a relationship or having sex. It's more about what you love on a day to day basis and how you can show your love for all things.

Don't get me wrong; being in a relationship is a wonderful thing and loving one can be a great thing as well. Just don't think that this is the only kind of love out there or the only kind of love that really means anything. Once you have looked at all the information there is to know and you have made your decision based on what you know about the person you want to have a relationship with, if you choose to have a relationship with them, stick with it. Make your decision to love this person for the rest of your life. I don't fully understand why people choose to be in a relationship with someone they don't plan on being with for the rest of their lives. In my opinion that is like taking a job you say you'd love to do, but once you're doing it, you find out you really don't love the job at all. That is why I want to make it clear to look at ALL the facts first before you commit to a relationship. You wouldn't go into a computer science field with no degree just because you love the pay, right? Then why would you go into a relationship with someone you would love to be with, but don't plan on committing to them? Love takes many forms but if your not willing to have the drive to love someone or something then you probably shouldn't be loving that person or job in the first place. You have to put 110% into loving. You cannot just say you love someone or something and not show it.

Knowing that you need to put 110% into your love will make you feel complete. In no way, shape, or form am I telling you what you should love or shouldn't love. It's simply how I found best to show my love for everything. It's not about what you love, but how much you love it that counts the most. People have the freedom to love whatever it is they want. Someone may love cherries and chocolate mint cake while someone else absolutely hates cherries and chocolate mint cake. The reality of it is, who cares what I love or what someone else loves. It's what YOU love that counts. At least here in America, we have the freedom to love whomever or whatever we want. So instead of worrying about what someone is going to think of you for loving whatever it may be, the heck with them. Love what you love and don't worry about what people may or may not say about you for it. I have been seeing it more and more on the news about gays and lesbians being bullied and pressured due to their way of life. That's something that just simply shouldn't happen. You wouldn't go up to someone and be rude to them just because they loved cherries or chocolate mint cake. Then why would you go out of your way to be rude to someone who is gay or lesbian? That is what makes America "America." We have the freedom to love without someone telling us it's wrong or right. So make sure you show respect to those around you who choose to love differently than you do!

Love is one of the most powerful feelings we can show throughout our day. Love takes many forms whether it is a relationship, love for work or a hobby, love for the ability to talk to your pet, or even the love to eat cherries or chocolate mint cake. By showing love you can inspire others around you to be or do great and wonderful things. Showing love should be a 24/7 thing that everybody in the world does (just imagine the possibilities). Being able to put 110% into love can give you a feeling of completeness and fulfillment. It's always best to show respect for those who choose to love differently than you do. It's what makes America so unique!

Education

personally think that education is the biggest issue we currently have here in America today. It seems as if no one takes education seriously, but more as just something that everyone needs in order to get a decent job. Education shouldn't be just about getting a decent job. It should be more about what you do in your field of study to make a difference in the world. The fact that other countries (like China) can put more focus on their education means that they care more about their future than we currently do. We would be able to solve a lot of issues here in America if we had people with better educations. Maybe that means building a better super computer, or finding a cure for cancer or AIDS. In my opinion the problem is there are more distractions in our lives that stray us away from achieving a great education.

I think the problem is in fact a distraction. It's not that we don't have a great education system or have lousy teachers and staff, but more children and even adults would rather do nothing than something. It's easier for people to play video games or watch television than read and learn. In my job as a substitute teacher, I have found that about 80%-90% of the students I work with either play video games, watch television, listen to music, or do very little at all. Now don't get me wrong; there's nothing wrong with any of that, but when you see children failing because they choose to play video games, watch television, or listen to music over doing their homework or studying, what does that make you believe in? Do you believe that it's the education system, teachers and staff to blame or the children? Neither!

I have found that people-children and adults-choose to blame someone or something else instead of taking responsibility for their own actions and choices. Now I'm not saying that people are always at fault or to blame. There are times when some technology isn't working right or a "mechanical failure" is to blame for the issue. With the education that people have the opportunity to get, people tend to blame the teachers, staff, or even the whole education system itself. Children don't understand what needs to come first, whether it's education or fun. They see how hard it is to learn and study while it's fairly easy to have fun. Again, I am not telling people how to be parents or how to teach their children at home, but when parents allow their children to do whatever, what can you expect? Children don't know any better unless they are taught. So when they go to school and learn their lessons in Science, Math, History, and English, then come home and play video games or watch television or even surf the Internet, do you think they are going to remember what they have learned that day in school? Chances are they won't and this is mainly because children know they have to go to school and they have to learn. They know that they can have fun when they get home. They are more likely to remember what they want to remember (whether it is a song, television show, or game). There is a time and a place for fun. There is a time and a place for learning and studying. There is too much fun spent in unstructured free time when children need to be learning, doing homework, studying, and learning good positive values. Fun is important, too, but our ever-changing world is not going to wait around for Billy to get done his video game so he can get a good education. Life keeps moving at a faster pace in today's world than ever before and life's not going to wait around for everyone to catch up.

Having expressed my opinion on the matter, who's responsibility (not blame and fault) is it for children having no boundaries or no responsibility when they come home? I hate to say it, but children learn from those they spend most of their time with from birth to teenage years. Since children are home for most of their childhood, that leaves it the parent's responsibility. Again, I want to stress that I am not telling people how to raise their children, but when they are failing or behind in school, it's not the responsibility of the teacher, staff, or even the education system when the children go home. To find out who's responsibility it really is when your children come home, you need to take a good hard look in the mirror because more times than most, children will learn from their parents! Let me give you an example. If someone out of the blue came up to you and gave you a million dollars and said, "Here's your opportunity. Do what you want with it." What would you do? Let's say you took that million dollars and blew it on alcohol, cigarettes, clothes, shoes, cars, etc. Would you blame the person who gave you the million dollars or yourself for squandering it away? You'd blame yourself because instead of investing the million dollars or even donating some of it to a charity, you blew it on meaningless possessions. So why would you blame the education system, teachers, or staff when they gave you or your children the opportunity of a quality education? If you feel this way, chances are it's because you blew your opportunity for a great education on having fun and not doing the work required. People need to understand that their education (whether you're young or old) is what sets your future up. It's literally priceless when you think about it. Your entire future is in your education and when people in our society don't get one or take advantage of the one they've got, they don't take responsibility for their choices. I have found people would rather blame someone or something else because it can't be their fault.

If I could give anyone a piece of advice it would be to go out and get yourself a good education! You hear it all the time. People who say that know what they are talking about. Knowledge is what's going to drive this nation forward. Without it we might as well stick a fork in us (as a nation). Be patient in your learning. Always ask questions when you don't know the answer. Above all, use your great education to create a better life, not only for yourself, but for everyone and everything in this world! Save someone or something. Inspire all. Show people it's okay to believe and take chances. Teach others the great and positive values you have learned in life thus far. You can do all of this by achieving a great education. Without it, you limit your true potential and abilities in life. Trust me, I know!

There is nothing wrong with our teachers and education system. It's how we use that service that determines whether we will have a bright future or not. Take responsibility for your actions and choices. Don't blame someone or something else for not receiving a great education. There is a time and a place for everything, whether it is fun or learning, so use your time wisely! If you do nothing else in your life, get a great education. It will help you to do wondrous things for yourself, others in your life, and everyone and everything in this world!

Addictions and Health

In this chapter I have combined both addiction and health. Originally I had the two topics as separate chapters, but I looked at the two chapters and thought "why have them apart?" They are both so closely related that I have kept the two together. Addiction is, in my opinion, something related to one's health (whether it is a positive or a negative).

An addiction can be one of the worst things in the world or one of the greatest. It is a little bizarre that such a thing can be either really good for you or really bad for you. Probably the most important thing to know about an addiction is knowing that you have one to begin with. From what I have seen, most times if you have a bad addiction, you are more likely not to notice it or dismiss the addiction (that is to say you tell yourself you do not have one). People need to confront their issues about their addictions if they are indeed bad for them or bad to others around them. However, as I have stated previously in this book, if there is a negative in life, there is almost always a positive as well. The same goes for an addiction. If there are negative addictions, then there must be positive ones. Sometimes if you have a positive addiction, it can be really motivating and inspiring (yes, as strange as that may sound).

Let's look at the obvious first. More times than not, if someone is talking about an addiction, chances are it is because the addiction is a problem. There are many different kinds of negative addictions including smoking, drinking (alcohol), gambling, stealing, killing, etc. Most times people will look at the negative addictions before the positive ones. Why is that? Simply because those people are more concerned about the negative addictions hurting you or your loved ones. People know that a positive addiction is not a bad thing and can actually help you as well as others around you. A negative addiction, however, is almost always going to affect you as well as the people around you. You may have an addiction and not even realize it.

Like many people, I have had addictions, too. When I had my first drink-a beer at 14 years old-I didn't think anything of it at the time. I was one of the guys at hunting camp. I was cool. Unfortunately and unbeknownst to me at the time, it would lead to a bunch of poor choices. You see when you drink, whether it is beer, a mixed drink, a shot, or a glass of wine, you start to lose sight of your senses and most times, you don't even fully realize what you are doing. You enjoy the free emotion you get and the carelessness it brings to your state of mind. You don't fully realize what you're saying or doing or how it is effecting you and the ones around you. There were a few occasions when I don't remember how I got from one room to another or had a total lack of remembering the night at all. I also recall times when I would be a little "buzzed." Other times I would be staring at someone, watching him talk, but would not be able to hear him, reply, or understand what was going on. This is something that was absolutely stupid for me to do and I share this experience with you so that you understand the consequences that come with making poor choices. Because I did this, there are great and wonderful memories that I simply don't remember anymore. You see alcohol kills brain cells and the more you drink, the more you forget and simply do not remember. The younger you start, the more memories you forget and the harder it is to concentrate on certain things in your future (like being able to achieve an education, remembering more of the memories you have made in the past, or simple tasks). So do yourself a favor when you do finally become of age to drink: if you do find yourself out on the town for a night or at a friend's house and you do start drinking, make sure you do a couple of things. Make sure the host has a general location for all the keys to all of the vehicles. I do not care if you have ten drinks or just a half a drink. You take that first sip or swallow-DO NOT DRIVE! If you're out on the town and you drove yourself, go to a hotel and get a room for a night or call yourself a cab. Don't ride with someone else who has been drinking either! Set a rule for yourself. Only allow yourself to have two or three drinks for the entire night. The more you drink and the faster you drink, the quicker you will end up on your butt flat out drunk. Also, do not go out with people that you do not trust. If you only met them that night or have only known them for a few weeks or even months, your best bet is to not go out with them at all. I have found you really don't know someone until you have spent a great deal of time with them. Remember, it's the choices that you make today that are going to shape your future. In other words, always make good choices!

Alcohol is not the only addiction I have ever had. As I said before, a negative addiction could be something as serious as drinking or something so simple that you don't even realize it is an addiction. I had an addiction to coffee that I didn't even know one could have. I use to drink pot after pot of coffee (about two pots of coffee a day) without fully realizing I had an addiction to it. In fact, I probably still wouldn't know about my addiction today unless my cousin's husband had not pointed it out to me in a weird way. Not so much as creepy-weird but more along the lines of out-of-the-blue-weird. He asked me the question, "So how's your coffee addiction going for you?" It was as simple as that. For the rest of that day I thought to myself, "Wow, do I really have an addiction to coffee?" So I started to look at the information in front of me and sure enough I come to the conclusion that I was indeed addicted to coffee. So much so that when I cut myself back to what I currently drink now (around a half a pot a day at the most), I got sick. I had headaches. I felt sick to my stomach. I couldn't imagine how people who were addicted to drugs or smoking felt when they quit cold turkey. They must have wanted to curl up and die. This just goes to show you that your addiction doesn't have to be a huge, big addiction for it to be an addiction. It could be the smallest thing in the world and to have it go unnoticed could still make it an addiction. The point is, make sure you can fully admit to yourself that you have an addiction. You hear people say all the time (whether they're joking or not), the first step is admitting it and the next step is fixing it. Trust me; it's the truth!

Now that you have some examples of negative addiction, let me explain (in my opinion) what a positive addiction is all about. It can be a wide variety of things, whether it is an addiction to love, charity, making good choices, over achieving, etc. The great thing about a positive addiction is that you don't have to worry about fixing it or changing your life style like someone who smokes or gambles. You can be addicted to laughing or helping people out at a food bank. There are many great addictions out there that will leave you better off than being addicted to drugs or alcohol.

Be careful not to get to addicted to "certain" positive things. Yes, even some positive things can leave you feeling empty and wondering, "What went wrong?" Take my dream of becoming a NASCAR driver. It was a personal dream of mine and a major career goal. In fact if you want to get technical about it, it was more of an addiction than the other two that I mentioned. Let's look at the facts. I was driven to race. I would do anything and give up anything to race. I spent loads of money to race, traveled great distances to be able to race, and most importantly, I was not honest with myself that I was addicted to my dream job of racing. My dream job was not a negative addiction because it wasn't hurting me or hurting anyone around me. I knew what I had to do to become a NASCAR driver, but that does not mean that this positive addiction (in the long run) was going to hurt me. In fact I put myself behind because of this addiction. Looking at it you can probably debate on whether it is indeed a positive or a negative addiction, but the fact that it was an addiction is still the same. The point is, don't get too involved with a positive addiction (whether it is work related or not) because chances are in the long run, you're more likely to hurt yourself or even worse, your loved ones!

There are two kinds of addictions: positive and negative. Most people focus on the negative addictions because those are the addictions that are more likely to hurt not only yourself but the ones around you. When it is said to you, "The first step is admitting it," chances are it is not a joke and should be taken seriously. By admitting that you have an addiction to begin with, you'll have better odds at being able to correct your addiction (no gambling pun intended). Not all addictions are negative. In fact there are probably more positive addictions than there are negative. You are better off being addicted to love or laughing than being addicted to drugs or alcohol. Never get too involved with a positive addiction because that can lead you to hurting yourself and possibly others in the long run. Above all, if you do go out on the town or to a friend's house to party or have a few drinks, DO NOT DRIVE!!!

Health can be considered one of the most important things we can understand and help ourselves with. I use to hear all the time, "I'm healthy for my age," from certain people who in my opinion were not healthy at all. They either smoked, over ate, drank alcohol, or did no physical work. It's surprising to know how many people are unhealthy, but still do not know or understand why that is. Or in some cases, believe that they are healthy when they have unhealthy habits.

Having an unhealthy habit is all it takes to start the ball rolling downhill. It could be something that isn't seen as unhealthy such as eating too much (or what I use to hear, "eating until you're full"). Say what you want, but in today's world there are more overweight people than ever before. Why is that you ask? With help from other unhealthy habits, one of the main causes is over eating or eating until you're full. Nobody should eat for something to do, just like no one should eat until they're full. For some I know this doesn't make sense and some people are asking, "Well, if I do not eat until I am full, won't I always be hungry?" Possibly, but here's my point. By not eating until you're full you are allowing your body to process the food from the three main meals (and any light snacks you have). If you eat to capacity at every meal, then you are making your body take more time to process the food you have consumed. In some cases, your body does not fully process this food before the next meal. Your body has to do something with the food it can not process and that is where the fat comes from. Your body stores this fat for when you need to use it the most and if you never need to use this fat, then it will just simply keep piling on. This results in an overweight person who is asking the big question, "How did I get like this?"

Another reason why people are overweight is from the lack of physical activity. Now if you were to ask anyone, I know they will all tell you the same thing. "This guy can put away food!" Yet I stay thin. How is that possible? The secret to my success in staying thin while being able to "put away" food is simple. I keep moving. What do I mean when I say "keep moving?" I never stop to sit around and be lazy. Maybe "never" was not the word to use, but I never stay in one spot for too long. I am always moving and doing something.

Whether I am working out or doing work around the house, I am always doing something. This is how I get my body to work more and process the food I have eaten. You hear how people burn off the calories or burn off the food that they had eaten. Well you don't do that by sitting on the couch watching television. You have to get up and keep moving. Go vacuum the house or wash the dishes. Go mow the lawn or rake some leaves. In other words, stay moving. Now I did mention working out and most people seem to think that they need to work out like a body builder in order to stay physically fit. In my opinion this is nothing but an excuse. By doing some form of work out (sit-ups, push-ups, jogging, etc.) two to three times a week, you'll be able to stay physically fit with no problem. But you have to want to work out. Look at it this way. You know that if you do nothing, you're going to put on the pounds. So why not do something? You're not going to stay fit or get back in to shape by just sitting on the couch drinking beer and playing video games. Get off your butt and go do something!

Being lazy and over eating are big issues for certain people who are overweight and unhealthy. However, there are many more reasons why a person is not healthy. I use to know people who took so many pills that it seemed like they had their own pharmacy! Yet they still said the words "I'm healthy." Take my word for it, if you're taking more than a couple of pills a day for certain problems with your body, then chances are you're not very healthy. Now I am not saying this is a bad thing. Obviously you need to take these pills in order to have some sort of healthy life style, but my point is don't say you're healthy. Understanding that you're not healthy will make you better aware of your issues and give you a better sense of being careful with your health. I admit that I wasn't always healthy and probably am not the healthiest person in the world or even the healthiest person in my own home town today. The point is I can admit that I am not the healthiest person alive. I know what my body can and can not do and what I should and should not do in order to keep my health up to its full potential. If I had to take medicine to keep my health up to par, then I would do just that, but I would understand I am not healthy. If I was healthy, I wouldn't have to be taking the medicine to stay healthy. Most people have done something in their past for this to have been brought on. Whether it was the person who started smoking or drinking or the person who over ate or continued to be lazy. My point again is to understand that everything effects your health on a day-to-day basis. Knowing what you should and should not do to your body can prevent issues to your future health.

Being healthy doesn't mean you have to work out everyday or eat right 24/7 (although that would not hurt you). You can work out like I mentioned above, two to three times a week and eat healthy about 75% of the day and be able to stay physically fit. By eating right, I don't mean eating until you're full or eating just fruit and vegetables either. I mean having a healthy mix of all your daily foods (protein, fruit, vegetables, grains, dairy, as well as the occasional candy bar). Doing that will be a great start to getting your health on the right track. That's not all you can do. You can quite any bad habits or addictions that you may have or have just started doing, whether it is smoking or drinking too much coffee. The key to staying healthy or becoming healthy is to acknowledge your bad habits or addictions and fixing them before they hurt you further or even worse, hurt others around you.

By staying or becoming healthy, you can live a longer and happier life. Being healthy and staying fit requires you to eat smart and healthy and always "keep moving." Just because you take medicine to stay healthy does not mean that you are healthy. If you were healthy, you would not need to take any medicine. It's okay to admit that you are not healthy but it is not okay to avoid admitting that you are unhealthy. Being lazy, smoking, drinking, playing video games, and unhealthy lifestyle choices are all ways to ruin your health. By working out, eating smart, eating healthy, and quitting any bad habits or addictions are all ways in which to stay healthy or become healthier. If you are one of the few that find good ways to stay healthy, then keep doing what you're doing. If you're one of those people who sit on a couch all day, drinking beer and playing video games, then some words of advice: get off your butt and go do something! You're wasting your life away!

Money

Doesn't it always seem that certain people have all the money they'll ever need and the ones who don't have money stay that way? Well there's a reason for that. People just simply do not know how to manage money properly. They would rather spend their money on meaningless possessions than save or invest in their future. Whether it's the everyday blue collar worker or the American government, it seems like they are spending not only all of their money, but money they don't even have. Sooner or later, this will catch up to those who continue to spend, spend, spend on practically nothing.

Now I'm not saying that taking a well-deserved trip here and there is a bad thing or buying something for your own personal pleasure is a bad thing either. It's how often you spend that is the problem. People spend way more than they probably make. This is why you always hear people complaining about not ever having enough money or how far behind they are on their bills. It's crazy to think about how much certain people make in a year and still have nothing to show for it at the end of the day. Let's say you have a house and a car, but you have standing loans on the two. That means you will be paying on them until they are paid in full (much more since there is interest on loans). So what happens if you lose your job or you get in an accident and are unable to pay these bills? After a few months, the banks will come and collect these items because you have not been paying them on time. So does that mean they were really yours in the first place? If you learn nothing else from this chapter know that until you pay the full price for something, it is absolutely not yours! You need to know how to manage money and invest properly so that you always have something to fall back on if and when you need it the most. A good start would be a Roth IRA or a 401k and continue to pay into it until you retire. Most times you start a 401K when you start working full time with a company that has benefits. That may not seem glamorous, but after you get your great education and have the job of your dreams, it will make it easier for you to save and put away for your retirement years. You also should start a separate account at a bank to save up for other life expenses, like a vacation every now and then. However, make sure that your bills are being paid (if you have any) and that your essentials are taken care of first.

What do I mean by essentials? Chances are unless you hit the lottery or invest in the stock market seriously, you'll have a mortgage and at least one car loan (unless you're smart and save to pay for one outright). Some other essentials would be food, gas (for your home, apartment and/or car), electricity, and any other utility bills that you may have. Maybe you have a pet. The dog or cat has to eat and drink. If you're in an apartment, you will most likely be paying an extra monthly fee to have your pet in that apartment. Before all of that, you'll need to pay to have your pet spayed or neutered. It also needs the recommended shots, flea and worm medicine, and whatever else is required. Now before you get too worked up and upset over the cost of living, understand that this is why getting a great education is so important. None of this is possible without one! That is why you hear about all of these young adults moving back in with their parents (including myself). It is because they get out of college and are unable to afford the cost of living. Most college graduates today do not get a job just like that and as a result, their bills start piling up. If this for some reason does happen to you, don't get down on yourself or feel depressed. That's just part of life and is why it's always good to have family and friends in your life. That's when you know who truly loves and cares about you!

Investing your money is what I have found to be one of the most important and riskiest things to do with your money. It's something that everyone should do, but should do in a smart and knowledgeable sense. Don't just invest money in a company or product that sounds good. You should really do your research on the company and/or product before putting one dime into it. I have found that investing in more than one well-respected company is the best route. I am not telling anyone to go out and put all their hard earned money in different stocks and bonds. This is part of being an adult and more importantly, an individual. It is about making your own choices and knowing that you will make the best possible choice with the information you have. As I mentioned, investing is both important and risky. One day you could invest $500 in a stock at $2.50/share (totaling 200 shares) and the next day the stock could drop to $1.25/share, leaving your $500 now worth $250. However, maybe after you buy your stock at $2.50/share, it goes up the next day to $4.75/share, now bringing your initial $500 invested to $950. No one truly knows what system of investing works (as there are many out there today), but everything in the world can and most likely does effect the stock market on a daily basis. Knowing all the facts about a company or product could make or break your investment. Chances are, however, you'll go to a stock broker to help invest your money. There are many different ways you can invest in today's world. My advice on investing is to know your information about everything you need in order to invest wisely and then double check that information! And by all means, NEVER invest all of your money!

I'll give you an example of poor money managing and good money managing relating to my own personal experiences. When I was chasing my dream of becoming a NASCAR driver I found that only two people were ever going to pay for my dream, either a sponsor or me. Since companies (or sponsors) want to invest their money in something that will make them more money than what they put into the sponsorship, my racing was all on my shoulders (financially). From 2006 to 2009 I was paying for everything I needed in order to achieve my goal of becoming a NASCAR driver. I first bought a truck for hauling purposes, then a 24-foot hauler, a racecar roll cage (minus engine, transmission, wiring, etc.). After I met up with a team from North Carolina, I found myself paying to race their street stock car at a local track in Hickory, NC. And all before this, I raced go-karts regionally in 2006 (the other expenses happened from 2007 to 2009) and I needed to pay for everything from the track fees, travel, to the go-kart itself. By the time I moved back to my home town (after I had lost the drive to pursue a racing career) in the beginning of 2009, I was over $40,000 in dept. My only option at the time was bankruptcy (which should only be used as a last resort). I had no secure job, no investments, no 401k or Roth IRA.

I have bounced back from that all-time low point and am now doing what everyone should do in the first place. Since I was previously spending money I never had, I now set some ground rules for myself. No more loans, no more credit cards, and no more foolishly spending money on meaningless possessions. That is when I started substituting at my local school. Having only minor bills to pay now, I find myself happier and wiser. You see, if you do not save and do not invest, then at the end of the day you will always be left with nothing. It's that simple. I had to finally come to realize that how I was handling and managing my money was foolishly. I had to grow up and make adult decisions with my finances. Knowing what I know now, I would rather have people learn from my experiences then go through what I had to in order to learn about managing money!

The most important thing we can do with our money is save and invest. If all we do is spend, spend, spend, then at the end of the day we'll always be left with nothing to show for our hard earned dollar. It is important that you understand the "cost of living" before venturing out on your own without a clue as to what's going on. With a good education, you'll be able to work at a job you love and be able to save and invest in your future. Investing your money is very risky and important so you should look at all the information about a company before investing and then double check it. It is ultimately your choice on how to invest and what to invest your money in, so take responsibility for your choices and make sure that you make the right choices! NEVER invest all of your money! If you lose it all on investing, then you are ultimately left with nothing! If nothing else, learn from MY mistakes on managing money so you won't have to go through the same experiences I did. You can thank me later!

Politics and Economics

It is important to know that politics and the economy are what drive America forward. Politics is one of the most talked about subjects in America today. Ultimately, the people in the U.S. government are the ones who make the political decisions to make a better life for all here in America (and sometimes in other countries as well). However, like everything in life, there are positives and negatives to politics too. I am no expert on the subject, so keep that in mind. Simply understand that this chapter, like all the others, is my own personal opinion on politics today. This chapter is meant to give those who are reading another opinion or view point on politics and should not be taken as fact.

So what about politics? Why do we have or need politics? Why are politics so important to everyday life? Well, from what I have gathered, politics is what makes America, "America". We are a country founded on a type of government that was different from all others, and based on individual freedom. We are basically the revolutionaries of France, Italy, Spain, England, and numerous other countries. Our main purpose for coming to the New World and starting our own country along with a new form of government and way of life is simple. We wanted to have the freedom to make our own choices and that freedom has allowed us to be who we are today. Without it, we could have been a country that today is ruled by England, Germany, Russia or even another country. We enjoy the freedom to be able to go out and get a job of our choice, eat what we choose, and live how we want to live. If I wanted to build a swimming pool, fill it with jello, and jump in naked, I could, simply because I have the freedom to do that (not that this has crossed my mind at all). The point is, without our democratic government, we might not have the freedom to do much of anything. We are so lucky to be partners of a political system that has (for the most part) treated us very well over the years.

Some of the decision-making on Capital Hill has been positive as well as negative (again in my opinion). I believe trying to find a better health care system so that all Americans are covered at low cost is important. I also believe that we should not have gone to war overseas. I am not saying that we shouldn't protect our country and our freedoms and I am certainly not saying that our military is involved in any wrong doings either. There is a time and a place for everything, including making military moves. I don't believe the right thing for America to be doing is spending billions of dollars on a war that is not on our own soil. It is important to protect our country, but when we have our military overseas and terrorists (like the hijackers on 9/11) are killing and injuring thousands of people in our own country, is that really protecting us? In my opinion we should not concentrate so much on international affairs, but make sure we can protect our own front yard. I believe that protecting America from within should be priority number one. If we can't accomplish that, then why spend billions of dollars on our military overseas to protect America? Once we can control the certain chaos within America, then I believe we can focus on other issues on an international level.

The politicians that run the government and make our political decisions on Capital Hill (and wherever else the decisions are made) should understand what a very smart man once said: A house divided can not stand. So why should that be any different in today's world? In my opinion, it shouldn't. There are too many people fighting and arguing about who's right and who's wrong, when there should be people in our government finding out what is actually the best route for America. If we the people of America can not trust or count on the people in our government to get along and focus on real issues instead of their own pride, then how does the United States government expect the American people to get along and focus on their issues that effect America? The answer is you can not. If the politicians on Capital Hill want the American people to agree with them and understand why they make certain decisions, then the people who make our important decisions need to start acting like "grown-ups" and stop the feuding between Democrats and Republicans. Who really cares who controls the House or the Senate? As long as both can get along, maybe there should not be any political parties at all. I can compare Democrats and Republicans to children with toys. If you have two children and one toy that they both want to play with, what happens almost 99% of the time? The two fight over who can play with the toy. Does that sound familiar? Sounds like the Democrats and Republicans fighting over who has power in the House or the Senate? Yeah, so maybe we need someone to make a new rule (or however it works). Maybe there should only be one name for the two parties and everyone work together so that the people on "Capital Hill" can make these important decisions instead of worrying about who's in power or if they will get elected next term. Or maybe there should be no political parties at all.

Personally, I am getting sick of political figures cutting each other down on television during election time. How many people can honestly say they have seen political advertisements every single day during election time? Sometimes I see or hear about people I never heard of before, let alone that they are running for election. After awhile, you start wishing you would see more car commercials or lawyer advertisements than political ones. It's sickening to see and hear what some political people will say about other candidates. These are the people who you vote for to make your important decisions? Personally, I wouldn't vote for some of these people for dog catcher in my own home town! In my opinion, I don't believe that cutting other candidates down is the way to the American people's hearts. I always vote for the candidates who choose to talk about themselves and tell the American people what they have done to deserve your vote. Not the ones who run down their opponent for saying something 20 years ago about something that has been over and done with for years. My advice to those who are reading this book that plan on running for a political position (whatever it maybe), don't focus your campaign on running your opponents down. If you want a good honest shot at the political position you're running for, be honest, tell the truth (even if it is bad), and above all, be true to your word.

It is important that as the American people we understand why the government does certain things and makes certain decisions, instead of jumping to the conclusion that they are making these decisions for their own personal benefit. We are a country that was founded on freedom to make our own choices. The people in our government should not be so divided due to political parties. The people on Capital Hill should work together and focus on the bigger issues instead of worrying about which party has power and whether or not they will get reelected next term. We should focus on protecting our own back yard instead of trying to fix other issues in other countries. Maybe the key to a more focused and better government is to get rid of the Democratic and Republican parties and work under one name (or no names) so there is no more distraction about who has power, who doesn't have power, or who is going to have power in the future. As a political person running for a position in our nation's government, be honest with yourself and the American people, tell the truth (even if it is bad), and above all, be true to your word. There is more than one way to look at politics (this includes your understanding as well, Mr. President)!

Another key objective in moving our country forward in the right direction is by having a sound economy. Economics is part of many things here in America as well as other countries. It involves the stock market, what we buy from other countries (imports), what we sell to other countries (exports), what we spend our money on, etc. All of these play a major role in the lives of millions of people each and every day. By understanding why the government might do certain things with the American economic system can help us better understand why certain things are the way they are (good or bad).

Understanding the system of imports and exports can be a confusing thing. I know that I don't understand a lot of the whats and whys of our imports and exports, but I do know this: I think we need to get the two straightened out. Let me give you an example of what I mean. We know as Americans that we can send people to space and we can build skyscrapers, but for some strange reason we can't manufacture our own toys for children, build cars, or even raise our own fish. I see more tools made from China or Taiwan than I ever see "made in the USA." We are the biggest "super power" in the world, but we fail to understand that we buy more and more common everyday stuff from other countries instead of producing the goods here in the good old US of A. I buy fish from one of the local supercenters and on the back of the package it says "product of China." I may buy a toy for my niece and on the tag is says "made in China." Why is that? Some will tell you that it is cheaper for American businesses to have their products built, assembled, or molded together overseas (whether it is in China, Taiwan, Bangladesh, etc.) instead of having all that work done here in America. Okay, so maybe it cost an extra three or four bucks to have the companies' products made here in America, but in the long run, who cares? Wouldn't you rather spend the money in your own country instead of spending it in another country? I know I would! If American businesses and companies had their products made here in America, they would be keeping their money here in the states instead of having it spent on employees overseas who don't come to America to spend money. American workers spend money in America. Chinese workers spend money in China. Then why have your company's products made overseas where you have to pay Chinese workers to make the product when you know that the Chinese workers are going to spend their money in China? It doesn't make sense, does it? At least in my opinion, it doesn't. It's really not hard to jump start the economy here in America again. If we had all the companies pull their production lines out of overseas countries and place them here in America (where they should be in the first place) and pay American workers to make the products, then wouldn't it make sense that the unemployment rate would go down? I hate to say this, but "DUH!" That way when these businesses pay their employees, that same money would be spent here in America instead of in some overseas country where that money might never get back to America. That wasn't so hard now, was it?

Another way to turn the economy around (again, in my opinion) would be to stop focusing so much attention on international affairs. This may sound stupid, but we pay too much attention to everybody else instead of ourselves. By doing this we are spending more and more each and every day on different operations or affairs in other countries when we should be spending that money on our own country. I can not tell you how many times I have heard how many billions of dollars America is spending on overseas military conflicts, whether it is in Iraq, Afghanistan, Korea, or another place. It's ridiculous when you know how much money we truly spend on things like this! We are trillions of dollars in dept (and climbing), but we still continue to spend, spend, spend. A good example of this is to look at what happened to me. I kept spending, spending, spending until I saw myself $40,000 in dept. What happened to me after that would be worse if it happened to America. I filed bankruptcy and lost most of my credit in the process. I had to start from scratch and build my credit back up to a respectable number (anything over 675 for a credit score is good). Can you imagine if America had to file for bankruptcy because we didn't stop spending? I'll tell you this much, we wouldn't be living as lavishly as we do now (whether you're rich or poor). Ultimately we would be in dept to another country (most likely China) and if it is anything like my bankruptcy, the USA would be losing things to China (property or assets). So America (in other words, the government who makes these decisions), let's wake up and smell the coffee. Let's stop borrowing and spending and start saving and paying back. Remember, it is never too late to do the right thing!

Economics may not have to be as big as the United States government but can be as small as your own personal finances. Our individual finances are so important that with all the spending that we do on a day to day basis, it also effects the overall American economy as well. If people understood that by saving, investing, and giving to charity, helps keep America moving in the right direction, I believe that they would be doing just that. But the fact still remains: people would rather buy meaningless possessions that really help them in no way shape or form. Buying things like beer, video games, movies, televisions, ect. just add up to a grand total of nothing. People don't want to hear that because these things bring them pleasure. Someone goes out and buys a 50-inch television set when they have a 42-inch television set at home. You ask them why they are buying a new one and they tell you, "Well I wanted something bigger to watch football on," or "I wanted something bigger to play my Call of Duty 3 on." No wonder many people are in the position they are today. They go out and buy all of these meaningless things for stupid reasons. Nobody needs a bigger television set or more video games.

So you can sit on your fanny and waste the day away? Sorry if I am sounding too rude or blunt, but I am so passionate about it because I know people who do this. I know people that blow money like it was nothing and then complain because they cannot pay their bills. Sound familiar? Sounds like our economy here in America. In my opinion, America blows money left and right and then complains because we are so many trillions of dollars in dept. You need to be an adult and make adult decisions, instead of blaming someone or something else for the choices that you made (whether we are talking about just you or America as a whole). I almost feel like a parent and saying, "You need to take more responsibility for your actions!"

The U.S. economy is one of the many driving forces here in America. Without a good economic system in place we will always be behind (whether we are talking about just you or America as a whole). Understanding our economics whether it is our imports, exports, stock market, what we spend our money on, etc. can make us better understand why certain things happen and why they do not. In my opinion we should bring all of our production lines from overseas countries and put them back here in America (where they belong). By focusing our money and resources on America instead of overseas affairs or conflicts is a good way to put money back in the country and turn our economy around. Economics can be as big as the United States government or as small as our own personal finances. Either way, if we blow our money on meaningless things, we cannot complain about not being able to pay the bills. We are not babies. We are adults and need to be taking responsibility for our choices when we use money. Let's wake up America!

Respect

Respect is one of the most important values we can show throughout our day. Respect can come in many different forms and through many different ideas. Respect towards others is thought to be the best form of showing respect (which it most likely is), but in my opinion, to show respect to others you have to first respect yourself. You're probably saying to yourself, "I respect myself. Why wouldn't I?" Most people don't respect themselves and don't even know it. They are right about one thing though. Why wouldn't they?

In a nutshell, people often look at their day-to-day lives and see nothing wrong with them. In most cases, people are right. For the ones who do not see how they act towards others and the ones who treat their own lives with no respect, they need to literally "wake up." It's not that those people don't want to respect themselves as well as others. They either don't see themselves being disrespectful (whether it is towards themselves or others) or just simply don't understand how to respect. It's actually very simple and you probably learned it way back in Pre-K or Kindergarten class. Some people even learned it from their parents. It is the simple act of treating others the way you want to be treated. That is the easiest way to show respect, not only towards others, but also yourself. What do I mean by that? Well, lets take a look.

Showing respect towards others is not hard, but sometimes confused with emotions or effects of other peoples' actions. In a sense, if someone is rude to you, chances are you're going to be rude right back (whether it is part of your character or not). A lot of people don't understand that being the bigger person and walking away (without the last word), is more times than not their best route to take. However, a lot of people feel as if they lose their pride by just ignoring the person or walking away without having the last word. Listen, your pride is something that you earn. Don't disrespect yourself by stooping down to their level. No matter how frustrated or mad you may be. Be the bigger person and just walk away. By doing that, you'll show the other person that you don't really care about what they had to say about you and you walk away with your respect intact. You see, people throw in the last word in order to get a rise out of you and make you do something stupid so that they have a chance to look better (and in some cases cooler). By being the bigger person and walking away, you show people (as well as yourself) how mature you really are and how respectful you are of others by not continuing the argument or problem. A lot of times my own family members did this. I would get involved in an argument with them and while I was trying to walk away they would throw in the last word. Since I was young and didn't know any better, I would turn right around and throw in my two cents and the argument would continue. After I learned that you show more respect towards yourself and others by just walking away, I did just that when I found myself in these situations. Don't get me wrong now. No one is perfect, but you can show great respect by taking these situations and turning them into a positive one by simply walking away.

Being able to show respect doesn't have to be just about being in an argument (although being respectful in an argument doesn't hurt), but more of how you treat others along with yourself. Treating others with respect makes for a great practice in being able to determine right from wrong. For example, is it right for someone to tell you that you shouldn't do this or that? Maybe it is. Maybe it's not. That's not the point. Being able to understand what they said and why they said it can show a lot more respect than just jumping to conclusions. By knowing what they said and why they said it, you can understand what made them say it in the first place. Let's look at the first part of that. A lot of people have a problem of hearing what they want to hear and not what was actually said. I have this same problem from time to time, but that doesn't stop me from being respectful. In some cases it helps me to be more respectful than if I actually heard the person right in the first place. Let's say you're a teenage kid and you were invited to a party by some friends of your friends for this Saturday night. You tell your mother where you're going and without missing a beat she says, "Well, I don't want you going to that party with those kids." Now it sounds pretty straight-forward, but let's look at what she is really saying. By saying "well" we know that your mother thought about it first (visualizing the pros and cons of you going to the party). The rest seems pretty clear, but looking at it closer reveals that she doesn't mind that you go to the party, but simply just not with those kids. In other words there's nothing wrong with you going to the party, but just with certain friends. Maybe your mother knows what those kids are like and doesn't trust them. Maybe your mother knows who their parents are and knows that there is going to be drugs or alcohol at this party. By being able to analyze her statement you can respect your mother more for being so thoughtful and concerned about your well-being instead of just jumping to the conclusion that she doesn't want you to have any fun. This also covers part two of my point: why she said it. Most likely your mother made this statement because she simply is concerned about your well-being and wants you to make the right choice. Yes, it's a party and it sounds like it would be fun, but being a teenager, anything sounds like fun and since your judgment may be clouded by thoughts of all the fun you'll have at this party, you forget that one of these "friends" has been in trouble at school. Maybe he or she was involved in a few fights and had you invited to pick one with you. Who knows? My point is by being respectful and trusting that your parents know best will better guide you in being able to have respect for your parents' decisions as well as understanding better decision-making.

Respecting yourself is a must if you plan on being able to respect others around you. If you don't respect yourself, how can you respect the people, plants, and animals around you? People who don't respect themselves tend to do things that hurt themselves (whether it is their self-esteem, health, lives, etc.) and sometimes that effects others as well. For example, if you were to get in a relationship with someone, but have already been in numerous relationships with people prior to this relationship, then how can you expect this relationship to grow? What I mean is by dating every Tom, Dick, or Harry (whether you're a guy or a girl), you show people that you have no respect for yourself. You're willing to go with anyone, no matter who they are, with no care or concern how this will effect you or your loved ones. Maybe you have children and they have seen you with five or six different people in the last two years. What kind of example are you showing your children by doing this? Now don't get me wrong. It's never too late to make the necessary adjustments to show your loved ones that you do have respect for yourself, but you have to understand how to do this. Unfortunately, this is one of those adult decisions you have to make on your own. No one is going to hold your hand through life and point you in the right direction. You have to be an adult and make these decisions on your own. Maybe the adjustment is staying single for a couple of years to show that you can live without a relationship. Maybe you choose to date one person for two or three years before taking your relationship to the next level. Whatever your adjustment is, know that you have to respect yourself before you can understand how to respect others around you.

Maybe your respectful by changing the subject or helping someone out who doesn't know how to do something. You could go out of your way to make someone laugh or rebuild someone's self-esteem after they had it knocked down. There are many different ways you can show respect and here is one of the best examples that I could give. The relationship I have with my grandmother (Mimay) is one of the best examples I can give. We don't always agree on everything and we sometimes bicker back and forth at each other (in a joking sense). The key I have found is that by acknowledging her opinion is the best way I can show respect. If we start talking about politics and she starts going on and on about a certain politician who she doesn't like or she thinks is making a poor choice, I don't tell her she is wrong. Instead, I agree with her opinion in the sense that maybe this politician is doing something wrong. Maybe she's right. Maybe she's not. The point is I show her respect by acknowledging her opinion about this politician. I may not agree with her and I can tell her that or maybe I do agree with her and still tell her, but by acknowledging that she has an opinion and wants to be heard, I am showing her respect. So if someone comes up to you and says, "You know you shouldn't have gone with Billy to the prom when you know I was going to!" simply reply, "You know, you're probably right. I am truly sorry for not knowing that you were going to take Billy to the prom." You are acknowledging that they have an opinion on who you took to the prom and that you honestly did not know until they confronted you. The alternative reply to that is most likely something along the lines of you saying, "Well it looks like Billy wanted to go with me instead." This can only be taken negatively and shows that you don't have respect for the other person's opinion. Instead, you're jumping to why Billy didn't go with her instead of apologizing for not knowing that she was going with Billy. Remember: be the bigger person and show the respect first. Most of the time this will lead to less conflicts and more people liking you for being respectful towards them.

Respect is one of the most important things you can show throughout your day. People often don't see themselves as being disrespectful (either to themselves or others) and simply don't understand why people treat or look at them differently than others. In my opinion, in order to better respect others, you must first respect yourself! You show others that you have respect for yourself and set a good example for the younger generation. One way of showing respect is by understanding why people say what they say. Don't just jump to a conclusion and get defensive about what people say. Really understand what they said and why they said it to begin with. There are many different ways of showing respect towards others. Acknowledge other peoples' opinions whether you agree or disagree with them (including mine!). Always be the bigger person and go out of your way by showing the most respect, even if the other person is a complete idiot!

Responsibility

One of the biggest issues in everybody's lives today is that too few take responsibility for their actions, ideas, thoughts, or beliefs. I admit that at times I am one who doesn't take responsibility and in a sense I take responsibility for that. You see, in today's world people cannot afford to look bad or be looked at for doing wrong. If somebody does wrong, more times than not, they will blame someone else or something else instead of taking the responsibility for themselves. There are many times when the problem or issue (whatever the case may be) lies with someone or something else and they need to take responsibility for their actions. All I am trying to make clear to you as a reader: you need to take responsibility for your actions no matter what they are.

Taking responsibility can be a great thing. By doing so it gives you a sense of ownership and better understanding of what works and what doesn't work. In some cases it may teach you a really good lesson on how to act towards others or treat others. Taking responsibility builds good character and even better values. People trust you more because they can rely on you to be honest and take responsibility for your work, ideas, actions, and reactions. It's not hard to take responsibility, but you have to know when you are in the right as well as in the wrong in order to do it correctly. Otherwise, you may take responsibility for all the wrong reasons and put yourself in bigger trouble than you realize. Understanding how to take correct responsibility is key to anything and almost everything you do. This is where your parents can come into play for real solid advice.

You probably hear your parents say, "You need to start taking responsibility for your actions!" Well, I am here to tell you they're not whistling Dixie. This is your parents being as real as they can be with you because when you actually get out there in the real world, people are going to hold you accountable for your actions and choices, not your parents. You see, your parents are not trying to "rain on your parade," but merely trying to get through to you so you understand that in order to have a successful life, you need to take responsibility for it. There needs to be a sense of ownership in your choices and actions and that is part of taking responsibility. This is one of those adult decision-making processes that you have to understand. Again, nobody is going to hold your hand and tell you what you should take responsibility for and what not to. You have to grow up and be the adult in your life and in this day and age, you have to grow up fast.

I'll see if I can give you an example that will help you better understand. Where I use to work there was a lot of paperwork to be filled out on orders, taking apart and putting together machines, taking product out of different areas and so forth. All of this paperwork had to be in order so the company could work efficiently. One "hiccup" in the paperwork and the company would fall behind on their work and ultimately, the company would lose money. In other words, you're on the hot seat! In this job I had to take responsibility for filling out the paperwork correctly, and since I was in production, I had to learn how to correctly take apart certain machines, clean them, and put them back together again. After that, I had to set them up on the correct settings as well in order to run them properly. Again, one wrong move and I was in the hot seat. I had a lot of great people teaching me how to do all of this. I had to take responsibility for my correct choices as well as my bad ones. By taking responsibility for my actions and choices I got more respect from my co-workers as well as the bosses of the company. My point here is that I was better off taking responsibility for my good and bad choices no matter what the case. Instead of trying to blame someone or something else for my choices, whether good or bad, I made the decision to take responsibility for all my choices and actions. By doing so I made a better work environment for myself and others.

Most people will tell you that they would rather be associated with someone who is responsible and reliable instead of someone who passes blame. Let's say you're one of the folks that takes responsibility and is very reliable, but you are friends with someone who is neither. Now what? I have heard an old saying which I believe goes something along the lines of "guilt by association." Yes, that's right. Even if you are very responsible and reliable, being close to someone who is neither can still make you look bad. That's not to say this person-whether they are family or friends-cannot change and make the necessary adjustments to be more responsible as well as more reliable. I have found, however, that more people get "burned" by just knowing someone who is unreliable, or irresponsible, and chooses to stay that way. It may sound cruel, but if that person makes it clear that they do not want to make that change for the better in their lives, then your best bet is to say your goodbyes and move on. I am not saying that you should disown your family or friends because they make a couple of bad choices in their lives. Everyone is human and we all make mistakes. But if this person has developed a lifetime habit of being irresponsible and unreliable, you're going to have to make that adult decision on your own about keeping that person in your life or letting him or her go.

Teaching others is one of our greatest opportunities as a human species! We are so advanced and knowledgeable that anyone in today's world can learn anything they want to and especially when we, have that freedom here in America. Being able to teach others (whether young or old) about being more responsible is a great value to hold and have in your own life. Teach people how to make better choices and take responsibility for their choices whether they are good or bad. By doing this for others, you'll show people that it is okay to make mistakes as long as they can take responsibility for them. It is a great gift to teach others as I have found through my substitute teaching. So use this freedom to teach someone the value of taking responsibility for their actions and choices!

Responsibility is one of the biggest issues that people have trouble accepting. It may be easier to pass the blame onto someone or something else, but it gives a greater positive feeling of ownership by take responsibility for your actions and choices. Your parents are most likely the best teachers of this great life value (as well as teachers at your school) so embrace this opportunity to fully learn why and how to take responsibility for your actions and choices that you make. Life is full of choices to be made and again, no one is going to hold your hand and point you in the right direction. Only you know your right direction. If you happen to make a bad choice, don't get mad or frustrated, but instead take responsibility for your choice and move on. By teaching others this great life value, you are not only setting your students up for great successes, but also giving them a great gift that they themselves will be able to reteach to others!

Safety

Safety is another important topic we can apply to our everyday lives. Being safe is not just waking up in the morning and making sure you don't bump into anything or making sure you don't do anything to hurt yourself. Being safe is to look at every aspect of your day-to-day life and say that you were safe at everything you did. Sounds like a lot and it is! It doesn't take a lot to be safe in everything you do, but more of having common sense and knowing what happens when you do something.

For example, if you were to throw a baseball into the air, you have to know where you're going to throw the baseball, right? Absolutely! You can not just throw a baseball into the air and expect it to go where you want it to. First, you have to look and judge where it would be best to throw the baseball. Then you have to think of how hard to throw it and how far you want it to go. If you do not throw the ball hard enough or far enough the outcome of where the baseball ends up is effected. This is the same process in judging how to be safe in everything you do. You almost have to be an investigator and analyze your day-to-day life and find the safest way through your day. Now there may be times where you just simply cannot avoid something and have to go with the flow. Sometimes certain things happen and whether they are good or bad, you have to adapt and overcome! You would love to avoid it or maybe even welcome it, but when it comes right down to it, it is what it is. By being as safe as you can be throughout your day, you set yourself up to have not only a good day but a safe one as well!

Safety and being safe can be applied to many situations in your life and how you react and approach these situations are ultimately looked at by everyone around you. Others look at how well you took on the situation and how safe you were. When I was in racing, safety was a big part of my everyday life. When you race pieces of equipment at high speeds for a living, you always have to apply safety to you life. Without being safe, for me it would have been life or death. I don't care if you're racing go-karts or stock cars. It is all about safety and you have to use your head and have some common sense. Driving around the track at high speeds, you have to know when to break, when to apply the gas, and when to turn left as well as right. Not all of racing is oval. In fact, most of my racing was on road courses with little time to hit the gas. I was always breaking, turning left, hitting the gas, breaking, turning right, etc. I had to learn how to be safe at high speeds. I had to make split second decisions with no room for questioning. At first, there were a lot of scared emotions where I thought "what happens if?" I learned you have to block those thoughts out of your mind in this sport and work from your gut and best instinctive decision. With no room for error, I learned and got better over time. Sure, there were times where I would spin or get in a wreck on the track, but as my decision-making process grew and grew, I had less spins and fewer wrecks. By applying safety checks in my mind, I automatically made quick safe decisions without second guessing myself. I'm not saying everyone should go out and race to pick up this skill, but you should find your own way to learn how to make safe (and quick if needs be) decisions on a daily basis. Sometimes your life, as well as other lives, could depend on it!

Sometimes there is no need for quickness in safe decision-making. There may be times where you have all day to decide and figure out which is the best and safest way to go about doing whatever it is you need to do. In my opinion, the quicker you go, the more likely you are to mess up. When you mess up, sometimes you put yourself as well as others, at risk. Now I'm not saying I make correct quick safe decisions all the time. It goes back to that old saying "nobody's perfect" and it's true. Not even machines are perfect, so why do humans have to be? You have to understand that accidents and mix-ups are going to happen and sometimes more often than not. You just have to be positive and continue to be as safe as possible. The minute you start looking at things negatively, the more negative things you'll receive in your life. Take it from me: be positive and safe throughout your day-to-day life. If something happens, just remember: you're not the only one. Chances are what happened to you has happened to someone else before and will probably happen to someone else in the future.

Now I'm not saying to look at life as one big giant question mark. You may not know it all, but if you know how to be as safe as possible, then you really shouldn't worry about anything. However, a lot of people look at life and think "it won't happen to me." I wish I could think like that and have nothing happen to me, but the reality of it is, thinking like that will set you up for disappointment when something does eventually happen to you. You shouldn't go through life being a coward and hiding all the time to be safe, but at the same time you shouldn't go through life thinking that nothing bad will ever happen to you either. It's nice to think that you'll go through life without any problems or issues, but life sometimes is not nice. In my opinion you should go through life knowing that life itself is not perfect. Understand that things will happen to you and your loved ones whether good or bad. By playing it safe, you give yourself a better chance at avoiding trouble and bad situations and leaving yourself with more good positive situations instead. You can apply safety to everything in your life, whether you are driving your car, teaching a class, playing catch with your child, or whatever you may be doing. There is nothing to be unsafe about. You can teach others how to be safe as well. Show someone how to do something the right way instead of the quickest way. Inspire someone to think of a safer way to do whatever it is they may be doing. There are many ways to show and teach safety to others around you.

Safety is a must in your day-to-day life. Without safety you risk hurting yourself and others around you. Although some people can make quick, safe decisions occasionally, most times it is better to be slow and safe than quick. By having the attitude of "it won't happen to me," it can actually set you up for disappointment when something does happen to you. You should look at life as not perfect and understand that things will happen (sometimes more to you than others). You should accept that life is not perfect and be safe so you can set yourself up for more positive days instead of more negative ones. Teaching others about safety is just as important as being safe yourself. By teaching others to be safe, you are making a safe environment for everyone. By applying safety and teaching safety to others in your day-to-day life, you are making a better and safer world for all!

Differences

In today's world, there are a lot of people bullying other people, whether they are white or black, gay or lesbian, smart or challenged, or whatever people find to judge others in a negative fashion. In my opinion, the bullies should take a good long look in the mirror and look at their own faults and issues instead of finding fault with others. I have touched on differences a bit and you can learn why people do certain things and above all, accept those people for who they are instead of finding fault with them. This country wasn't built on freedom for certain people only, but freedom for all!

Recently in the news it seems like there are a lot more stories about kids being bullied for whatever reason. More and more of today's children are under bigger pressures compared to even several years ago. When I was in school there were no social networking sites or kids taking photos with cell phones. I remember in my mother's classroom where the computer screens were black with green lettering. That was back when all of this social networking was in the thought processes and even when cell phones with cameras were just being introduced. Today's children have more opportunities to be friends with millions of people over the internet. With that comes great responsibility for these children. But we have to remember: they are children, not adults. Most children don't have the respect or responsibility to know what they do or say on the internet can be seen by millions. So when one kid is bullying another, there is greater damage done when they have the opportunity to put embarrassing photos, videos, or comments on the internet for others to view. Most of the time (from what I remember from school) kids who bully other kids usually do it because they have their own issues in their lives and cannot handle whatever issues they may be. As a result, they pick on and bully other kids to make themselves feel better and forget their issues. In a nutshell, these are kids who are not mature enough to take on their own issues and would rather cause problems for others. They figure that if they cannot be happy, then why should others. I am glad to see that the law is enforcing a "tighter leash" on these bullies because from what I am seeing on the news, there are more and more kids thinking of suicide because of the problems of being bullied. What should these kids do?

Thinking negatively about being bullied is not the way to go about it. As stupid as that sounds, think of all the positives that come with bullying. You now know that one of the main reasons for bullying is because the bully has bigger issues than you. Maybe you can tell your school counselor or principal that this individual may need help. Understanding that the bully is immature and not able to tackle his/her issues gives you more reason to notify an adult about the individual's behavior so they can find out the root cause of the behavior. Other positive thinking towards bullying is helpful, but not effective if you keep it to yourself. Tell a teacher, principal, or counselor at your school about it, even if the bully does not go to school. Tell a police officer or anybody that can help you and the bully as well. The bully is a person with conflicted feelings. Chances are the bully has something bothering him/her and doesn't know how to handle the issue. Not everyone is a psycho, but by all means, do not keep the bullying to yourself! Nothing will be taken care of until someone who can do something about it knows about the situation. Don't be scared to do this because you feel that other people will not be able to trust you for turning someone in. In fact, you are just trying to help. Ultimately you shouldn't worry about what people may say or think about you. The only one you should make happy at the end of the day is yourself.

If you are worried how people may view you or talk about you no matter what your race, religion, sexual orientation, etc., I am here to tell you, you're wasting your time. In my opinion you should be spending your time working at other things that are positive instead of worrying. I am one to know. I use to worry about everything from looking cool, talking to women, looking smart, etc. What I came to realize is as long as I am happy who cares about what people may think of me? Why should YOU care about what people think or say about you? You shouldn't and that is what I believe people worry over more than anything else. People worry about trying to look good or being cool to impress people. You don't have to be cool or look good in order to impress people. How about making a difference to impress people? I can guarantee you that if you were the one to save a baby from a burning building, no one would care if you had one eye, half an arm, or were gay. People would be more impressed that you saved a baby, not how well you looked doing it. Those people who talk or think badly about you are actually more jealous of you than you are of them. They wish they could have been there to save a baby from a burning building to look as cool as you did. Now I am not telling you to go set a day care on fire so you can look cool saving babies. I am telling you not to worry about how you look or act. Everyone is different in this world with no two people the same. Just imagine if everyone was the same. It would be pretty boring, wouldn't it? So understand that it is okay to be different and accept you for who you really are. If you can't accept yourself for who you are, how is anybody else going to?

For those who choose to bully people for being different, you should take a good look in the mirror because chances are you have bigger issues than most other people. Accept people for who they are. No two people are the same, so why pick on them about being different? You should understand that people are different for a reason. Maybe someone is gay or lesbian because they are attracted to the same sex. Maybe there are two people who are dating each other who are of different races. Maybe someone has a missing arm because they lost it while seeing military action overseas. Again, is that any reason to be picking on them or bullying them? No! You don't have to be in school to be a bully either. There are more people in the work force today that are bullies than there are in schools. Nobody, including the bullies themselves, are benefiting from what they are doing to others. Instead of bullying, why don't you spend your time helping out at a local food bank or donate your time to charity? Use your time better instead of wasting your time finding fault with others!

We can all do a little better at accepting people for who they are instead of picking on them. At times, I look at myself after I have made a comment about someone or something else and realize that it was me picking on that person or thing. I usually give myself a smack on the back of the head as a wake-up call, to make myself realize that I should not have done that and take responsibility for my comments or actions. If you find yourself doing the same thing, don't get down on yourself or feel bad. Simply correct your wrong choice. Nobody is perfect and nobody expects you to be. Just take responsibility for your choices and actions. Go apologize to the person for your poor actions or comments. Maybe you could make him/her an offer to help out with something he/she is having a problem with.

People should be respectful when they talk to or about other people and acknowledge their different thoughts and opinions. You should make people laugh who are feeling down about themselves or teach someone something that they did not know. Show people love and affection, who on any other day would not receive such a gift. There are many positive things you can do that will make people simply forget about how different they are and how much alike we all are. If nothing else, make the better choice!

It is not only terrible to bully, but unfair to others who are dealing with their own problems. If you are a victim of bullying, the worst thing you can do is think and act negatively. Instead, tell someone (a school official, teacher, police officer, etc.) what is going on because if nobody knows about it then nobody is going to help you to fix the problem. Chances are the individuals who are bullying have issues in their own lives that they cannot handle or are not mature enough to do so. By trying to get them help, you are not only stopping the bullying, but you're also helping the individual as well. You do not have to be in school to bully or be bullied. More people worry about trying to look better when they should be focused on how to be a better person and make a positive difference. When you think about it, who really cares what people may think or say about you? At the end of the day, you should be happy for who you are and not for how people may view you. By accepting others for who they are and understanding why they are the way they are, you can be more understanding and respectful of their differences. If you find yourself bullying or picking on someone or something, then accept and take responsibility for your actions and choices and make things right! There are many positive things you can do to make a difference in the world today. Use your time to make a positive difference in your life and the lives of others instead of finding fault in others for their differences!

Loyalty

Perhaps the best way to describe loyalty is that it is the end result of all the values in this book (if not more that I may have forgotten). Being able to say that you're loyal to whatever you may be loyal to is simply saying that you have applied one or more of the values in this book to your own personal life. You may be loyal to your parents or your studies. You can say that you have loyal friends or pets. You may even say that you have been loyal to your job or goals that you previously set. You have to be loyal to whatever you have or want in order to receive it or keep in in your life.

Let's say that you are loyal to your job and want to keep it. You are always to work on time (if not an extra five to ten minutes early). You show respect to your bosses and co-workers. You always do your best job possible, taking responsibility for your actions and choices while on the job. By doing these things at work, you show your bosses and co-workers that you are reliable, trustworthy, have a great knowledge in the work you do (educated), that you have a drive to do your best each and every day, and that you also have a passion and love for the work you do. To achieve this maybe you are always educated in the work you do. Maybe you have learned to pace yourself so that you know that you will always do your best work. You show that you have great patience for your work and when things go wrong, you think positively. You believe and have faith in the work you do and always give your best. You do your work in a safe manner and stay healthy so that you can think about the work with no distractions. You enjoy your work and make everyone around you laugh and love their work as well. You can see how almost all of the values in this book are tied into just your work. This is how you become a loyal person. You apply the values of respect, responsibility, patience, safety, positive thinking, love, etc. There is no limit at the different combinations you can make with these values.

Let's say you respect your parents' decisions and take responsibility for your actions or choices. Your parents trust that you know how to take responsibility and understand that you respect them for their decisions. By showing your parents respect and responsibility, they now trust you more and love you more for it. You don't have to use all the values in this book in order to receive all in return. You'll find that sometimes you will show a couple of the values and receive one in return (as the example with your parents). As long as you can hold on to those values, you'll never lose them. You'll only gain more and more!

At my last full-time job, I always did the work to the best of my ability showing responsibility for my actions and choices (whether they were good or bad). I was respectful towards my co-workers and the bosses as well. I understood their opinions as well as their differences (whatever they were). I showed love for the work and a drive to do my work to the best of my ability (not just for the pay). I did my work as safely as possible knowing that it would not only effect me, but others around me as well. I joked around with co-workers who were feeling down or sad just so they could laugh and enjoy coming to work. I always tried to think positively even when I didn't want to. I was patient in my work so I knew that I would give 110% every time. I found a steady pace to do certain jobs to know that they would get done on time and get done right the first time. Above all, I believed in my work and had faith in myself that the work was done to the best of my ability. By applying almost all of the values in this book to my everyday work life, I became a loyal and valuable worker within the company and had a great work experience along with a terrific work environment because of it.

Now I am not going to lie to you and tell you that I applied all of those values every single second of every single day. I am human just like everyone else. Nobody is going to expect you to be perfect 24/7 so don't expect to apply all of the values in this book to your life 24/7 as well. I had bad days just as I had good days and still do. I simply applied those values as much as possible everyday that I could and I did not apply all of them every single day. You don't become loyal overnight. You have to work at it and show the people around you these values as much as possible. Only then will you become loyal to the ones who see you as such. Again, not everyone may view you as being loyal. That is where everyone is different and has different views. As long as you apply these values as much as possible to your day-to-day life, you'll know that you are loyal and others will notice it, too. Just don't get your hopes up that everyone will see you as being loyal because this is not the case.

I look at certain people as being loyal and others, not so much. That is my opinion and that is what makes me different from you and everyone else on this planet. It is what makes some people interesting and some people seem like complete idiots. No two people are the same. As long as you can accept that and understand that not everyone you encounter will view you as being loyal, you'll be just fine. Remember that by applying these simple life values, you're not only setting yourself up for successes, but also allowing people to see the real you and not someone who is doing certain things or acting a certain way just to look cooler or look important. Important people are not the ones that go out of their way to look or act cool. They're the ones who make a positive difference in the lives of others (whether a big difference or a small difference). People will view you as being loyal to the positive differences you make in the lives of others. So what are you waiting for?

By applying all of these values, you will be viewed as being loyal to whatever it is you are applying these values towards. You don't have to apply all of these values each and every single day, but by applying as many as possible throughout your day, you will set yourself up for successes as well as having people view you as being loyal. Not everyone is going to view you as being loyal, but if you apply these values you will know that you are loyal and some others will notice. Important people are not people who go out of their way to look cool or be cool, but they are the ones who make a positive difference in the lives of others. As a result, people view those important people as being loyal for their positive differences that they have made in the lives of others.

Life & Death

P robably the most asked about questions in all of human history are either about life or death. In my opinion, the reason for this in my opinion is that we just simply do not have the answer to two main questions. The first question is what happens to us before we take life in a human form? The second question is what happens to us when we die? We simply do not know and not because we are not smart enough to know but because we choose to think of it as a complex answer. Who really knows? Maybe it really is a complex answer, but I believe that some of the biggest questions in life have the simplest answers. In both life and death we know one thing to be true and that is they both happen. More importantly you cannot have one without the other (meaning you cannot have life without death or death without life). It simply would not make sense.

Let's first focus on life itself. Why does life happen in the first place? That answer I cannot tell you and if you were indeed expecting me to give you the secret, then you simply set yourself up for disappointment on this one. I am no scientist or mathematician with all the right numbers to punch in to give you the answer you were looking for, but maybe we can learn something from this. Maybe life itself is not ever meant to be answered, but simply lived. Look at it this way. You are here (same as me) whether you like it or not and you will remain here until you simply die. I am not telling you or anybody else to go kill yourself or another so you can find out the answers to life, but just simply stating the obvious. If someone or something is alive, sooner or later it will eventually die. That is just simply part of life. Nobody gets out of life alive. I have never heard of anyone or anything escaping or surviving death. Everyone and everything lives and dies (one way or another). I am not trying to be a downer, but that is the reality of life.

That is why I stress in this book to do positive for not only yourself but for others around you as well. We only have one shot at life so why mess it up by wasting your time or acting in a negative way? If everyone asked themselves what **really** is important in life instead of what they **think** is important than I believe everyone would enjoy life a whole lot more. In our lives, that **really** is the big question: what's really important? We have to look at our lives, evaluate them, and make decisions based on our evaluations. Should I go out and party tonight and drink heavily? Or should I spend some time with my grandmother in her final years of life? Let's say you choose the first option. You go out and party most of the time instead of spending that precious time with your grandmother. You enjoy yourself but you overlook your grandmother's aging life and eventually she passes away. Now you find yourself sad and miserable because you come to realize that you wasted your time partying instead of taking that opportunity to spend that time with your grandmother. You think to yourself, "if only I had more time," but the reality of it is you had all the time in the world and blew it partying. Yes, this is very sad and depressing, but I want to get my point across. You may have chosen the second option and spent that precious time with your grandmother during her last years on Earth bringing meaning to her life. You need to realize the reality of life and understand what really is important! Nobody is going to tell you to spend time with your grandmother. You have to go out and take that opportunity while it is there in front of you. This example is very depressing but maybe this will open your eyes and mind up to what really is important in life instead of what you perceive as important.

Maybe you are a parent and have three children and do not want that life style of being a parent anymore. You want to go capture your youth and go back to "enjoying" your life the way you use to. So you leave your family and everything you once held close to your heart and decide to go recapture your youth. Five years goes by and just like in the last example, you come to realize what you gave up on and missed out on. Maybe you missed out on watching your children grow up or miss the laughter and joy that your family once brought you. You end up finding yourself wishing you could go back in time to relive those memories. You come to realize that you cannot and you have to live with the choices that you have made. My point is you have to know what really is important in life instead of what you think is important. Maybe life was entering a rough patch and you wanted the easy way out and to go relive your youth again, but that does not mean giving up everything either. Look at my own life with my dream of becoming a NASCAR driver. I gave up practically everything to pursue racing no matter what, including what I held dear to my heart. I missed out on what would have been some great memories and yes maybe some bad ones as well. Like everything in life there are always going to be positives and negatives. I now realize that that was no excuse for me to give up everything and go. Sure I made some great memories, but I also lost some great opportunities to spend time with the ones that really meant the most to me. I cannot say it enough: understand and accept what really is important in life instead of desiring what you think or perceive is important in life. Trust me, you will live a better life because of it!

Life will throw some curve balls and you have to know how to get back up after being knocked down by life. In my opinion, if you get knocked down by life and do not get back up, then you will have ultimately been defeated by life. What do I mean? I told you how I moved out of state to pursue a relationship at a younger age (21 years old), giving up everyone and everything in my life only to find out that I gave up everything for nothing but a lot of heartache and misery. Having been knocked down, I picked up some bad habits and made some negative choices. At this point I could have made two choices: to either continue down my negative path or by simply changing my negative life into a positive one. Remember: you can have only two outlooks in life, a positive one or a negative one. I could have let life win and keep me down for the rest of my life or I could have changed and gotten back up after being knocked down. I chose to get back up and move on and that is my point. Life will have its challenges and you will have to experience these challenges in one way or another. It's whether you get back up after being knocked down and move on with your life that's important. Nobody is going to hold your hand through life. No one is going to be next to you 24/7 telling you to go down this road and not that road. You have to realize that life can and will be challenging at times. You have to simply face reality and move on no matter what the situation is. Knowing that life is better looked at as positive than negative is a great start! Understanding and accepting life and all that it has to offer (whether it be positive or negative) is a must to get through life's challenges. There are many challenges to tackle and it is ultimately something that you will have to figure out as you go through life.

Understanding time is key to everything in life. It can save yourself a lot of disappointment, frustration, sadness, and many more negative feelings. You see, everyone has the same amount of time. There are always twenty-four hours in a day, seven days in a week, and three hundred sixty-five days in a year. We all have the same amount of time in life, but it's what you do in life that determines how much of it you really have. You will most likely end up with less time if you smoke, drink, do drugs, or whatever else may cause a human life to fall short of one hundred years. There are things that can help a human live well past their prime of one hundred years like eating healthy, staying active, and making good choices. My point is you control how much time on this Earth you have and the choices you make will either better your chances of living a longer life or weaken your chances at that longer life. I hear people all the time saying, "there isn't enough time in the day" or "this day is taking forever." I hate to break it to you, but it is all how you look at it. In my opinion if you are asking yourself these two questions (or questions similar to these two) then you are most likely thinking in a negative way. If you were thinking in a positive way, you would not complain about not having enough time or having too much time. You would simply look at it as always having just enough time. There are some people that just do not understand that by looking at something in a positive way it will give them positive results. If you view your time as negative, then you will end up having negative results of how you view your time (whether it is in your day, your year, or your life).

Give yourself enough time to get something done and done right. Make sure you do not set yourself up for disappointment when looking at how much time you have on this Earth. Simply look at it as "I will have all the time I need to do what I need to do on this Earth." Do not feel disappointed if you find yourself getting closer to death and realize that you have not done something you wanted to do or feel that you missed out on some great things in life. Chances are there are some people that will look at their own lives and feel the same way about certain things that YOU have done. Not everyone is going to accomplish everything in life so it would be foolish to think that you could. Understand that you used your time wisely in life and you have done things that many will never get the opportunity to ever do. Accept that you will not accomplish everything there is to do in life and accept that your life was worthwhile! Simply understand and accept that everyone has the same amount of time on this Earth as everyone else and that by using your time wisely and productively, you can make a better world for not only yourself but everyone else around you!

If you do nothing else in life, teach someone life's great values! There is nothing more important you could do. Teach someone how to be respectful and responsible. Teach someone the value of being honest and being able to trust yourself first. Be the first to teach and understand that the teaching starts with you. Without you initiating the teaching of life's great values then how will anyone know about them? Children (and even teens and adults) simply will not learn and that is why it is important to be the first person to teach someone about life's great values. If I was never taught how to laugh at my mistakes then I would be laughing at everyone else's mistakes. As a result I would not realize that I was being disrespectful towards others all because no one took the first step in teaching me that you should laugh at your mistakes and not someone else's mistakes. You can teach someone one of life's great values and not even know it. I do it all the time when I'm substituting. I go into a class acting like myself (as professional as possible) and show the students that it is okay to be yourself, enjoy school, and learning as well. There are days when I do not even know I am teaching them to just be themselves or understand peoples' differences. It just happens, but again I am taking the initiative and giving myself the opportunity to teach others life's great values. So go out and present yourself the opportunity to teach someone one or more of these wonderful values of life!

Life may not have an answer to the question "what happens before life?" It is important to understand what really is important in life instead of what you may think is important. Life is full of challenges that everyone will have to face in one way or another. It is not important at how hard life knocks you down, but it is important whether you get back up and move forward with life after being knocked down. Understand that we all are given the same amount of time on this Earth and that it is important to use that time wisely! If you do nothing else in this life, teach someone life's great values so they can make this world a better place for all of us to enjoy!

Now that we have talked about life, let's talk about death. Death is the one thing people in today's world fear the most. They worry about not only how they will die but more importantly what will happen after they die. You see, since we do not have the answer to the question "what happens after life?" we are fearful of simply not knowing. I have gotten headaches over this question and trust me, it is not fun to think about. You worry about not only what will happen to you but your loved ones as well. Let's look at why death happens in the first place. You cannot have death without life or life without death. Otherwise we would just live forever (which in my opinion would be pretty bad). You see, if we lived forever then we would always have pain, suffering, disappointment, and many more negative feelings. However, we would also have positive feelings as well like love, happiness, along with many more. This is where the value of believing and having faith comes in. If you do not believe that things will be good and positive after death then you will simply always believe in negative thoughts about death. Remember, you can think of things either positively or negatively, but not both. So if you plan on living a worry-free life, then your best bet is to think about life and death in a positive fashion. No one person will cheat death so it is better to accept the fact that all people will eventually die and move on. That is not to say that there isn't life after death. Many people believe that we go on to different lives after death, but it is simply all how you look at it.

There is really no preparing for death. It may come in the next five minutes or fifty years down the road. The point is that you need to make sure that you live your life to the fullest each and every day. By doing this you will feel more accomplished and when the time does come, you will have the feeling of no regrets and simply accept death. How you treat your body, what your life style is, what kind of choices you make, along with many more decisions can determine whether you live a long good life or a short miserable one. When the time comes (and if you're able), do not feel bad or negatively about not having that much time left. Simply accept that death happens to all of us and teach others that it is okay to accept death in every way, shape, or form.

I know that when someone first passes on from this life, it is really hard to accept especially if it is a loved one. Once you lose a loved one it is going to be hard to go through the first few days, weeks, or even months after their death. Life is not easy (by any means) and you will be faced with challenges including death of loved ones. You have to understand that death happens to everyone and everything. Accept death when it comes (whether it is death to a loved one or your own). Do not feel like you have to hold back the tears to be strong or that it is not okay to cry or feel sad. In my opinion, the strongest people are the ones who are not afraid to show their emotions, including sadness with tears. So do not feel as if you have to hold yourself back in order to be strong at the loss of a loved one. Cry, mourn, shed the tears, and move on with life. No one is going to think any less of you and if for some reason someone does, then to heck with them. Those are the people who do not know how to handle death and have to find fault with someone else in order to look better or look as if they are stronger than you. When it comes right down to it, who cares what anyone else thinks of you? The only one who should be judging you at the end of the day is you! Understand however that everyone handles death differently than you do. Not everyone may be as strong or as emotional as you are to death and you should always show the utmost respect to people when they have lost someone close to them. Be there for them. Show them it is okay to cry and show their sadness. Show them that it is okay to move on and not to feel guilty by moving on. In other words, do something positive for someone or even yourself after dealing with a death of a loved one.

Moving on with your life is a must. By not moving on you will always be in that depressed state of mind. That is why you must understand that death happens to all and that it is okay to accept a death and move on. Moving on requires you to do so at your own pace. You may move on with your life at a faster pace than others while someone else moves on with life at a slower pace. Just know that whatever pace you move at is okay! Do not feel as if you have to rush through the emotions that come with a death or that you have to move at a slower pace. Your pace is simply your pace of moving on after a death and nobody should be telling you otherwise. This is something that you will have to figure out on your own. Someone may tell you to move faster or slower with regard to the death. You have to figure this out on your own and unfortunately the only way to learn is to go through the emotions of dealing with a death of a loved one. I really do wish I could give you better advice to go and learn how to pace yourself with moving on with your life after a death, but it is all a part of life. No one said that life was going to be easy and sometimes the best learning process is to actually experience it for yourself so you know what you can and cannot do emotionally. Listening to others tell you it is okay and listening to words of advice and encouragement is always helpful. Just do not get caught up with people telling you "you have to move on." This is one of the worst things you could do to someone who has just lost a loved one. When I had this happen to me, I felt as if I was being pushed or forced to get through my grieving at a faster pace, all because someone said the words "you need to move on with your life." It is good to encourage someone to move on, but do not come across sounding demanding when you say these words. You will most likely have people who will dislike you for it. Do something positive to help others deal with a loss (as well as yourself) and always remember that everyone moves at their own pace.

Remembering loved ones who have passed on is something everyone should do. I do not believe it is healthy for your state of mind to try to block someone who has died out of your mind. It could lead to other issues along the road of life. I am not saying to build shrines in honor of them but maybe put some photos of them up (preferably photos with them smiling or showing how much they truly enjoyed life). It is better to remember the ones who have passed on for not only who they were but how much joy they brought to the lives they came across. I had a close friend and someone who I considered a brother that passed on about a year or two ago. At first I was sad, but he was so much fun to be around and he brought so much laughter to my life that no matter how much I tried to mourn or grieve his loss, I just simply could not. All I could do was hear him cracking jokes (whether it was about his life or not) and remember how he made everyone around him enjoy life. I don't really know how to put it into better words than that. I believe my point is that you have to find the best in people even after their death. Remembering someone for the joy they brought to the world can either be easy or hard on you. As long as you remember them for the joy they brought to your life and the lives around them, you will be just fine.

If people don't know how to deal with death, then they will most likely stumble through the process (whether it is dealing with death or trying to understand and accept death). Be the first to teach someone how to deal with death. Show them that it is okay to show your emotions whether they cry or not. Teach someone how to understand and accept death. There are many important ways you can go about showing and teaching about death, but it is pointless unless you actually go out there and teach someone. If people have more than one opinion or outlook on certain things, including death, then they will be able to compare and come to their own conclusions. If they are shown only one process or taught only one opinion about death, then they will only have that one outlook on death. Go out into the world and teach someone the understanding and acceptance of death.

As long as there is life there is death. No one gets out of life alive so sooner or later everyone will face death in one way or another. There really is no preparing for death, but just accept that it happens to all. It is always okay to show your emotions whether they include tears or not. If you cry at the loss of a loved one it does not make you weak. It makes you strong. The strong will not be afraid to show their true emotions at the loss of a loved one! Everyone moves on after a death at their own pace and should not be rushed or told how to mourn or grieve. Do something positive to help the ones who have just lost a loved one instead of finding fault with the way they mourn their loss. Everyone is different and by being different, everyone mourns, grieves, and moves on at their own pace. Remembering the loved one you have just lost is a good way to keep a healthy state of mind. Remember the good positive times that they brought to your life and the lives around them. It is important to teach and show someone the understanding and acceptance of death. If you don't know how to understand and accept death, you will stumble through the process. Be the first to teach and show someone the importance of understanding and accepting death!

Making Good Choices

Ultimately this is what we all want to accomplish in the end. Making good choices is something that we really do not have to try too hard to do throughout our day, but is something that we, more times than not, fail to accomplish. This can happen to good people or bad people, well-intentioned people, kind and caring people, or even down right rude and crude people. In other words, it really doesn't matter who you are. It's more of how you look at certain people and situations in your life that determines whether or not you make good choices.

People often ask "why do bad things happen to good people?" Well first of all, bad things happen to both good and bad people just as good things happen to both good and bad people. The choices you make today ultimately makes the person you will become tomorrow. Knowing this will help you to better understand how important it really is to make good choices as much as possible. Now I am not writing that you have to donate all of your time to charity or to a good cause, but more of flexing that time to fit both into your day. Making good choices isn't just about deciding whether or not to have the diet soda or not, but more of how you go about your day making a positive difference in your life and the lives of others around you. You wouldn't go up to a homeless person and rob them. You would probably go up to a homeless person and give him a few bucks so he can get a meal. It seems pretty obvious as to which one is the right choice. Taking a better look at the example can hopefully make you better understand that choices that seem good may not always be good choices. Let's say you walked up to this homeless man and gave him a few bucks. Before you even do this you have to ask yourself the question "what made him homeless to begin with?" This may not be an easy task since there could be countless people who are homeless in the area. Let's say that this person is one of twenty homeless people in your area. Now that should make it easier since you know that a company recently went out of business and a few hundred lost their jobs because of it. You know that this person is homeless because he lost his job when the company he was working for shut down. So in this case you probably made the good choice. However, who's to say that he wasn't the one who got his company to close its doors to begin with? What if this person sabotaged the company and was the reason now hundreds of people are out of work? What if this person is not even one of the people that was fired from the company but just someone passing through your town? All good questions that you should have an answer to before you go giving a few bucks to a complete stranger. The well-intentioned thing to do is to give the homeless person a few bucks, but what if this person sees all the hundreds you have in your wallet and is someone who is homeless because he has had run-ins with the law? I don't like saying "what if" a lot, but sometimes you have to get the answers to make your good choice. This seemingly harmless homeless person could very well follow you home and rob you in the middle of the night not only putting you at risk but your family and neighbors as well. The point I am trying to get across to you is to simply think things through before making your choice (whether it is to give a few bucks to a homeless person or whatever it maybe). You can envision the different outcomes from the choices you have.

I know a few years ago I would have loved to have this ability of "thinking things through," but sometimes people have to learn certain values by living them. This was the case for me. Don't get me wrong; both my parents always said "be responsible and always make the better choice." When 2008 began, I was just getting involved in a relationship. Once the two of us had spent time with each other (over a two to three month period), I felt as if I had found the person I was suppose to be with for the rest of my life. I was looking at starting a family and raising children. Whatever was involved with having a family life, that was what I was driven towards. Not racing, not anything back home, but only this. With this mind set, I had made the choice to move out to the state where she was and pursue this drive of starting a family with the one I loved. I gave up everything from my racing dream, to my job, my family, and basically my way of life. I proposed and we were looking towards a wedding that fall or the following year. She had become pregnant within this time and decided that we didn't want a wedding. That seemed like "we're only getting married because we're pregnant." One week in June (right before Father's Day) I not only found out that our unborn baby girl had Turner Syndrome (which meant we had to kill the pregnancy), but my fiancé didn't want a relationship with me as well. Before I go any further, let me say that this is my personal opinion of what had happened and don't blame myself or my ex-fiancé for the events that had come to pass. If I had made the right choice, I wouldn't have put myself into this situation in the first place. By simply having one mind set and basing my decision on that mind set, there was only one choice for me to make. If I had looked at all the information, been more responsible in my decision-making by envisioning all the different outcomes of all the choices that I had available to me, I would have narrowed it down to the best possible choice. Instead I made a choice that was well-intentioned but by no means the best choice for me at the time. I gave up my dream of racing (for a time), my family that I had grown with and who have taught me how to make good choices (which I overlooked), my job (at the time I left I was making around $20.00/hr with full benefits including a 401k), and ultimately my way of life. After all of this had come to pass I did make a good choice.

Before I packed up and left the life I had moved so far to achieve, I stayed an extra, month and a half. You see, I could have just left and hit the highway, but I didn't want to just pack up and leave. I had so much time, money, heart, and love invested that I wanted to make sure that I left my ex-fiancé in a good state of mind. I looked at it this way: I was not by any means the only one effected by the events that took place in 2008 and in my opinion the poor choice would be to just leave my ex without knowing she would be all right. Yes, we still had fights and we still said things to each other that we both probably should not have said, but that didn't mean I still did not care about her or cared if she would be all right. There were points where I had to leave and stay at a friend's place because the tension was so high. But I stayed anyway and made sure that my ex was indeed going to be all right. After what had happened I did have issues and found myself at times depressed, addicted to alcohol, and even having suicidal thoughts. You've got to remember, I had my life invested in this relationship, gave up everything, and within a week and a half's time, it all fell apart without notice. Being 21 years old and trying to accept all that happened and understand it all so fast, it's just something that didn't happen. That is most likely why I fell into a depressed state, having horrible thoughts and becoming addicted to alcohol. No one said it was going to be easy. If life was easy, nobody would hurt or have bad days. The reality of it is, life is not easy. Life is full of all-time highs and very low lows. In 2008, I had my all-time high of loving life and my all-time low of wishing I wasn't even there anymore. Nobody is going to hold your hand through life. You have to be an adult, understand the pros and cons of every situation and take responsibility for the choices and actions you make. That's all a part of growing up and sometimes it takes highs and lows to make people understand and fully appreciate what they have. We are in a country where we have the freedom of choice. We can choose to do whatever we want. We have that freedom. Knowing the effects of your choices and the consequences of your choices is something people have to understand as well. Back to my story, I stayed an extra month and a half because I cared about my how my ex was going to fair as a result of what had happened. I may not have liked my choice and may have even damaged my own situation by staying in that environment longer than I wanted to. But sometimes we have to do things we don't like in order to help and make sure others are going to be okay (whether they know it or not). Making good choices doesn't always have to be about you. Making good choices can also be about making them for the people around you as well.

If you were to walk down the halls of my local school where I substitute and ask the students there what is the one thing you hear Mr. Greco always say, I believe you would hear the response "Mr. Greco always says make good choices." I say it so much that sometimes I'll be in a class and I start to say "You know, this wouldn't have happened if . . ." and before I can get it out of my mouth, the students will say "We know, if we make good choices." We laugh about it and have a better day because of it. I try to teach them that by making good choices they never have to worry about making a bad choice again. In my opinion, it's that simple! Could you imagine if everyone in today's world only made good choices? No one in the world would ever make a bad choice again. Imagine what kind of world that would be where everyone made good choices. However, this is not the case in today's world. People only want to make the choices that will only benefit them the most, not fully realizing the effect their choices have on others around them or even others they may have never met before. You have to fully understand the effect your choices will have. By doing that, you'll be able to fully understand your choices and ultimately make better ones.

By always trying to make good choices, we'll have a brighter future for not only ourselves but the lives we effect. Just because it may be the right thing to do doesn't mean it's the best choice. To make a good choice we have to fully understand the effects it will have on us and on others. We have to envision the outcome of each choice before we can make a good choice. By understanding and learning from others, we can look at our own lives and situations and better understand how to make a good choice instead of a choice based on our mind set. Making good choices does not have to be just about making them for you but also making them for the people around you as well. We may not like it but sometimes we have to make good choices that may effect us in a negative fashion so that they will effect someone or something else in a positive fashion. That if you do nothing else, teach someone that by making good choices, they will be able to make a positive difference in their lives and the lives around them!

Ending Remarks

n life you will be faced with highs and lows. You will meet new people and say goodbye to others. Always think positively about every person, situation, and experience whether it is truly good or bad. I have found (in my short 24 years of life) that if you think in a negative way you will almost always receive negative results. Whereas if you think in a positive way you will almost always receive positive results. You will not always be blessed with good and you will not always recieve the bad. Understand that by thinking positively and by applying good values to your everyday life, you will almost always set yourself up for successes. Not everyone in life will like you for who you are and sometimes, they will treat you like crap for no reason at all. There will be some people who will treat you like gold, teach you important things, and show you how to teach others around you. Know that at the end of the day, the only one who should be judging you is you. You make the right choices for not only yourself but for others around you even if it effects you in a negative fashion. Know that not everything in life is about you and that others are the way they are for a reason. It is important to respect people for who they are and respect yourself for who you are. Understand that there is indeed something bigger than you out there and accept that. No one is perfect and no one expects you to be perfect either. Accept responsibility for your actions and choices. Respect and understand that when you're wrong, you're wrong. It is okay to admit when you are doing something wrong as long as you attempt to seek help in fixing your problem (whether it is an addiction or whatever it maybe). If you do nothing else in life, learn, understand, and apply these great values and teach them to others around you. Most importantly, remember that "nobody gets out of life alive" so use your time wisely! We all have the same amount of time whether we are talking about time in a day, a year, or a lifetime. It's how we use this time in a positive way that makes all the difference!

I want to express how truly thankful and grateful I am for having you, the reader, take the time to read and hopefully understand this book. It shows that you are looking to improve your life as well as the lives around you and that is ultimately what this book is all about. This book is about my own opinions on different values that we should apply to our lives on a daily basis. By reading this book, you've shown that you are interested in knowing how to understand these values as well as how to apply and teach them to others. Hopefully you understand why these values are important to everyone. Remember, it's the choices we make today that make our future of tomorrow. If we make good choices today, then our future of tomorrow will look brighter than ever! Thanks again and may God bless you on your bright and shining future!